The Library's Continuous Improvement Fieldbook: 29 Ready-to-Use Tools

Sara Laughlin
Denise Sisco Shockley
Ray Wilson

American Library Association
Chicago 2003

The paper used in this publication meets the minimum requirements of American National Standard for Information Sciences--Permanence of Paper for Printed Library Materials. ANSI 239-48—1992.

Library of Congress Cataloging-in-Publication Data

Laughlin, Sara, 1949-
    The library's continuous improvement fieldbook : 29 ready-to-use tools / Sara Laughlin, Denise Sisco Shockley, Ray Wilson.
      p. cm.
    Includes bibliographical references.
    ISBN 0-8389-0859-4
    1. Library administration—Handbooks, manuals, etc. 2. Total quality management—Handbooks, manuals, etc. 3. Library administration—United States—Case studies. I. Shockley, Denise Sisco. II. Wilson, Ray, 1942- III. Title.
Z678.L34 2003   2003010432
o25.1—dc21

Printed in the United States of America.

07 06 05 04 03   5 4 3 2 1

Contents

Contents

Foreword

Libraries are facing significant challenges such as budget reductions, increasing expectations for new or improved services from patrons, constantly changing technology, and new workforce demographics. It is not business as usual (as if it ever were). Faced with all those needs, what's a library to do? Beginning in the 1980s, many American businesses realized that they had to revitalize and do it quickly. W. Edwards Deming and others led the way in showing Americans—and others around the world—a road map for how to rethink the way work should be done.

Deming pointed out that all work is made up of processes. Libraries are very process-intensive organizations. These processes can include everything from ordering materials and cataloging and circulating them, to preparing story hours, scheduling meetings, preparing budgets, and on and on. Processes are the meat of libraries. Processes are what customers or patrons see. One of the ways for libraries to remain relevant and vibrant institutions is to pay attention to how library work gets done. This does not mean hiring an army of consultants. It means training and empowering the staff to improve processes.

We have been involved with helping libraries and other organizations change for many years. We both had the honor to work at the American Productivity and Quality Center at the time the Malcolm Baldrige National Quality

Award was created. We remarked then that someone should write a book on how to do continuous improvement in libraries. Two decades later, the continuous improvement literature still is overwhelmingly dominated by books focusing on the manufacturing, business, and education communities. The team of Ray, Denise, and Sara brings formidable collective experience with libraries and continuous improvement to this book, which is long overdue and sorely needed.

Change is hard and people don't like to take on challenges that they are not sure they can meet. Library professionals and staff members need to know not only what the tools of continuous improvement are but, even more critically, how they will produce results. Like many others, librarians love tools and approaches written in their own language by people who understand them. This book will reassure them, since it is written in their language by people who have worked in and with librarians using the tools. The stories have the ring of truth.

The trio of authors of this book have made learning to apply the tools of continuous improvement not only palatable but also interesting. Most of us love a good story and reports of success. The format used here will appeal to most libraries. We recognize that all libraries are different, but at least the reader knows that these tools work. The examples the authors cite are often projects based on their direct experience. This is not a do-as-I-say-and-not-as-I-do book.

Not all the tools must be applied exactly as described in the book; most are ones that library staff can have some fun adapting and making their own. These are not the only tools, but they do work and are easy to use. This book is not about applying the approaches perfectly. It is about engaging the hearts and minds of all library staff to make a difference, not only for patrons, but for their own sense of satisfaction.

Remember that continuous improvement is a group sport, so use this book with teams where possible. It's not as if many staff members haven't said, "There has got to be a better way to do this." And they are right! Buy multiple copies of this book. Then tell your stories to Ray, Denise, and Sara. They would love to hear from you. Have a great time and bon voyage!

SHARON AND DAN WISEMAN
Chicago, Illinois

Preface

This book was created out of *frustration* and *hope*.

Frustration because more and more often we are being asked as consultants to help organizations answer the question: "How are we doing?" We believe that the questioning will only intensify over the next few years, as the demand for accountability reaches libraries along with every other public agency. Funders and policymakers will be interested not only in *inputs* (like budget, buildings, staff), and *outputs* (like circulation, gate count, web hits or program attendance), but also in *outcomes*. They'll want to know if the library is adding value to the community or organization, if it is making a difference in customers' lives, and if it is improving and becoming more efficient.

During several years of working as consultants doing strategic planning in libraries and other organizations, we have witnessed exhaustive (and sometimes exhausting) efforts to create plans which were submitted to an external agency and then shelved to gather dust, while the library went on doing what it had always done and therefore continued to get the results it had always gotten. We began to suspect that it wasn't the plans or the planning, but the inertia of the system that kept anything from changing.

We looked around, and although there are examples of continuous improvement aplenty in the business and education world (and even in some government arenas), we found few ex-

amples and no comprehensive models in the library world.

Hope because, in 2001, we invited a handful of Indiana public libraries to help us develop such a model, based on W. Edwards Deming's philosophy of continuous quality improvement. We were pleasantly surprised by the level of interest and participation; at this date, teams from nineteen libraries have completed the eight learning sessions. The results far surpassed our expectations, as libraries:

- Began to adopt a new systems-thinking paradigm for improving library operations
- Used tools for getting their staffs involved in making team-based decisions
- Developed baseline data to answer accountability questions
- Included customers in their improvement efforts
- Began to see some initial improvements from their actions
- Formed a network for continued mutual support

Continuous improvement tools are available in scores of publications and on dozens of web sites. It is our hope that this volume will provide a valuable addition for libraries that wish to join us on the continuous improvement journey, with its easy-to-use collection of tools and the success stories that paint vivid pictures of how the tools have been used in real libraries. We have some initial evidence that they work, based on our observations and feedback from participants in our early sessions, including one who commented: "This has...given us tools we can use in many ways."

Another wrote: "The CI methodology has changed the entire climate of our library system for the better. It has been enormously helpful in boosting morale, unifying purpose, spirit and attitude among staff in all departments and both facilities."

And a third added: "Just when I thought I didn't have anywhere to go as a director, along came CI for Libraries. Now I feel that the challenges and opportunities for making a difference at my library are limitless."

If you use the tools and they work, we'd love to hear from you. If you know of other tools that help people work together, using data, to improve library processes, we'd love to know about them too.

SARA LAUGHLIN
DENISE SISCO SHOCKLEY
RAY WILSON

Acknowledgments

We couldn't have written this book without support and pressure from many people. We especially want to thank the incredible teams from the Indiana Library Federation and the nineteen Indiana public libraries who assisted us in developing the learning sessions, tried out the tools, kept us focused on the realities of real-life libraries, and graciously consented to let us include their stories in this volume:

Avon-Washington Township Public Library
Bedford Public Library
Benton County Public Library
Bloomfield-Eastern Greene County Public
    Library
Brownsburg Public Library
Carmel Clay Public Library
Delphi Public Library
Dunkirk Public Library
Huntington Public Library
Jeffersonville Public Library
Kendallville Public Library
Lawrenceburg Public Library
Mooresville Public Library
Peabody Public Library
Plainfield Public Library
St. Joseph County Public Library
Thorntown Public Library
Union County Public Library
Wells County Public Library

Thanks also to Ann Delehant, Rochester, N.Y., who contributed tools and her experience, and the many books, articles, and web sites that contain descriptions of continuous improvement tools in use in business and education contexts.

For their love and patience with our protracted and boisterous meetings in all three kitchens and many late dinners and Sunday-evening absences, we thank our families: Sara's husband, Tim, and children, Isaac and Hannah; Denise's husband, Richard, and faithful dog Carmen; and Ray's wife, Cindy.

Intern Elizabeth Lewis made the original page design.

Joe Lee learned about continuous improvement tools in order to create illustrations that bring the concepts to life.

Cindy Wilson and Donna Rinckel gave us the valuable gift of editing.

We are standing on the shoulders of W. Edwards Deming and all his disciples, who have so enriched our understanding of systems and people. To all of them, we extend our deepest appreciation.

Mistakes and omissions, of course, belong only to us.

Overview of Continuous Improvement

It all began for some of us in the United States in June 1980 when NBC News televised a White Paper called "If Japan Can—Why Can't We?"[1] This TV show focused our attention on what we already knew—that Japanese electronic products and automobiles had the highest quality in the world. It introduced us to a man named W. Edwards Deming, and it initiated many pilgrimages to Japan to try to find out what made the Japanese manufacturers so successful.

And like the proverbial blind men who inspected different parts of an elephant, we all came home with different views of the secret to success. Some of us saw quality circles, which we translated into teams and more teams. Some of us saw lots of graphs with numbers and dots on them. Some of us saw the karetsu system of interrelationships between manufacturers, suppliers, dealers, and government, which struck us as unfair, uncompetitive, and un-American.

But regardless of what we saw or thought we saw, some of us were desperate enough or courageous enough to try something. We gave different names to our attempts—statistical process control (SPC), quality improvement, continuous improvement (CI), Total Quality Management (TQM), zero defects, Total Quality Leadership (TQL), kaizen, total quality control. Some of our efforts were successful and some were dismal failures.

Those who persevered realized that this was going to be hard work, and it was going to be a lifelong journey and not a program or event. Many who continued began learning from Dr. Deming in his famous four-day seminars, which he conducted all over the world until 1993. In those seminars and Dr. Deming's books, we began to get a grasp of what we needed to understand and do.

We learned that an organization, whether manufacturing or service, is not an isolated entity but is part of a system that includes suppliers and, most importantly, customers. We learned we must listen to our customers and surprise and delight them. We grasped that at least 90 percent of our problems within an organization are system problems and not people problems—where we most often placed the blame for failures.

We learned that building quality into our processes and products at the beginning is much more efficient than correcting problems at the end. A Harvard Business School study in 1980 concluded that the more quality, the higher the productivity, the lower the cost.[2] We established that, on average, in any organization 30 percent of our time and resources are wasted.

We realized that managing an organization involves making predictions and that, in order to make predictions, we need data. We learned that there is variation in all people, products, services, and processes, and that if we can reduce variation, things will be better. Using the data we can get clues as to how to track and reduce the variation. We grasped that, even though the first, and perhaps the easiest place to apply continuous improvement was in the manufacturing area, the same techniques, tools, and philosophy worked in non-manufacturing areas. In fact, Dr. Deming often mentioned that the biggest gains would be made off the factory floor.

We learned that employee involvement is critical to success. Employees can only be successfully engaged if they know where the organization is going and the ground rules they must live by. Successful organizations do this by communicating their aim or constancy of purpose—mission, vision, values, and measures. We became sensitive to the fact that employees know their jobs, and the frustrations associated with doing their jobs better than anyone else. If given the opportunity, they will make things better.

In the last few years of his life, Dr. Deming summarized what he had learned and what he was teaching as a theory for management called the System of Profound Knowledge, which is composed of four parts:[3]

Appreciation for a System

On a basic level a system is composed of individual tasks and processes. When related tasks are linked together to transform inputs into outputs it is called a process. And when related processes are linked together to accomplish an aim, that grouping is called a system. We have found it helpful to think of a system as a mobile with many individual elements. When you picture the mobile, it is easy to see that if any individual element is changed by a gentle breeze its relationship to all the other elements and its surroundings is now changed. So, too, is a system, an organization, changed when any element of it changes. A leader's job is to optimize that system.

Knowledge about Variation

It is important to understand that processes can be stable and therefore predictable. The process can be stable whether it has a large or small amount of variation. There are also processes that are unstable and therefore unpredictable. It is very important to understand the difference and to make decisions accordingly. It is always best to bring processes under control and to reduce variation. This requires taking measurements and using data handling tools.

Theory of Knowledge

We are inundated with facts, ideas, and information. These are not productive to us until we turn them into knowledge. Knowledge requires us to have a theory. When we have a theory or make a prediction, we can learn. One of the ways we can learn is to employ the Plan-Do-Study-Act (PDSA) cycle. We can plan (have a theory), do (try it out), study (evaluate the results), and act (decide what to do with what we learned). Importantly, an unexplained failure of a theory is a significant opportunity to learn. As Myron Tribus said, unless you gain knowledge and learn, "You do not accumulate thirty years of experience; you just have one year repeated thirty times."[4]

Psychology

People are a key component of any organization. People are different from one another. They learn differently, have different aspirations and different abilities, and communicate differently. People want relationships. They want to be part of a successful team. They want to feel like their contributions are valued and make a difference. They want to be challenged, and they want to have some control over their work life. They want to be part of something bigger than themselves. We must recognize and accept this. We must learn to optimize the talents, interests, aspirations, and energy of everyone. There are well-established methods and tools available to do this.

Smart organizations are learning to apply the new management theory and to use their largely untapped employee resources to improve. Unfortunately, it isn't as simple as decreeing, "Go do it." It takes learning and change on the part of traditional management and investment in training of employees. Over the past twenty years we have learned that teaching and using "continuous improvement" tools are essential. When employees have the basic CI tools mastered, they can think, communicate, and analyze issues with confidence and efficiency. Their organizations see significant gains in employee involvement and operational improvement.

The tools included in this book are well tested. They have helped hundreds of organizations understand their systems, reduce variation, improve their knowledge and understanding, and optimize the talents of their people. Because we know that many of them are also foreign to libraries and their traditional approaches to planning,

management, and decision-making, we have included stories about real successes in real libraries with each tool.

Because "a journey of a thousand miles begins with a single step,"[5] we urge libraries to take the first step and try one of the tools right away on an existing set of data, problem, or with an existing committee. We have seen over and over that the results can be transformative. Meanwhile, understand that the study of continuous improvement is a journey of more than a thousand miles. Endlessly challenging and rewarding, both personally and professionally, it may become a lifelong quest.

Notes

1. W. Edwards Deming, *The New Economics for Industry, Government, and Education* (Cambridge, Mass.: MIT, 1993), 94-118.
2. Lloyd Dobyns, "If Japan Can—Why Can't We?" (Wilmette, Ill.: Films, Inc., 1980), videocassette.
3. David A. Garvin, "Quality on the Line," *Harvard Business Review* (September/October 1983), 65-75.
4. Myron Tribus, Deming Electronic Network, at http://deming.ces.clemson.edu/pub/den/archive/90.04/msg00162.htm
5. Attributed to Confucius.

Choosing the Right Tools for the Task

The continuous improvement tools included in this volume have a number of uses and can easily be combined to increase their impact. The chart on page 6 clusters them into their most common uses. Sometimes, in fact, the tools are so interdependent that they have minimal impact if used alone; they must be used in combination or in sequence in order to have maximum benefit. Other tools are so widely applicable in so many contexts that we are constantly amazed and delighted to discover libraries making use of them in ways we never imagined.

We have endeavored to situate the tools in real library contexts in two ways.

First, a success story is included with the description of each tool. Although the stories are designed to illustrate that particular tool, we often refer to other tools and include the page numbers so that the reader can easily locate more information. The success stories come from real libraries, most of which have participated in our continuous improvement training series, from the training sessions themselves, and from other libraries where we have discovered their successful use of the tool.

Second, in the chapter following the individual tool descriptions, titled "Using the Tools in a Continuously Improving Library," three stories illlustrate ways that many tools have been used together to address real situations in real libraries. Some situations had existed for years; others were emerging challenges. The tools gave the libraries a chance to "reframe" the situations, so that they were viewed not as problems but as opportunities for improvement. In each of the three libraries, the people who did the work made improvements in their own processes. They and their supervisors were amazed at how simply and quickly they were able to make the improvements, a tribute both to the effectiveness of the tools and the willingness of the library staff members to participate in experimenting with changes.

We know that the uses we have imagined and documented are only a partial representation of all that are possible. The libraries we have worked with have constantly surprised and delighted us with new combinations and new applications. We continue to find descriptions in the literature of continuous improvement that suggest different or more sophisticated possibilities. As businesses, hospitals, schools, and state and local government adopt the practice of continuous improvement, libraries are sure to find others in their communities who are learning about and applying the tools and with whom they can share experiences.

Use of the tools must be situated in the context of the organization. This is often the most difficult hurdle to get over when introducing tools to an organization for the first time. As practitioners, we have begun using a tool in an appropriate situation only to discover, by the body language and nonparticipation of others in the group, that they were not about to "play that silly game." As facilitators, we have experienced several instances where the culture of the organization is so strong or rigid that an outsider cannot easily influence it. In some cases it is almost as if we are invisible when we say, "Let's do a Plus/Delta to evaluate our meeting." Individuals continue talking or putting their coats on to leave.

Using a tool for the first time can be unsettling. We have discovered—from our own experience and from the libraries with which we have worked—that, even though it seems straightforward when you are reading the step-by-step directions for using a tool or working with a teacher, the first time you actually use the tool on your own or try to teach it to others, you may discover complications.

You may have these difficulties introducing the tools into your work situations. Our best advice is to practice using the tools in a safe place, with a trusted co-worker, with a group that likes to try new things, or with a newly organized team that hasn't set its culture in concrete. We hope the explanations and examples given for each tool will give you confidence to give them a try. Our advice is to practice using the tools. We know that the more you use them the better you will get and the more valuable they will become.

"Most people are too busy working to get their jobs done."
—Brian Joyner

Tool	Choose among alternatives	Clarify responsibility	Develop consensus/ reach agreement	Encourage participation	Find root causes of problems	Gather data to study processes	Identify and organize large amounts of information	Improve efficiency/save time	Present information visually	Reduce large or complex issues to manageable size	Run efficient meetings	Stimulate creative thinking
Affinity Diagram			x				x	x	x	x		
Agenda								x			x	
Brainstorming				x								x
Cause Analysis	x		x	x	x		x			x		
Cause-and-Effect Diagram				x	x		x			x		x
Charter		x		x				x			x	
Check Sheet				x		x	x					
Consensogram			x	x					x		x	
Criteria Rating Scale	x		x	x			x					
Fishbowl				x								x
Flowchart: Deployment		x		x	x		x	x		x		
Flowchart: Top-Down				x	x		x	x		x		
Force Field	x		x	x	x		x	x			x	x
Gantt Chart		x		x			x	x		x		
Group Norms			x	x							x	
Histogram					x	x	x		x	x		
Multivoting	x		x	x			x			x	x	
Nominal Group Technique	x		x	x			x			x	x	
Operational Definition			x	x			x					
Pair and Share			x	x			x					x
Paired Comparison	x		x	x								
Pareto Chart						x			x	x		
Parking Lot				x			x				x	
Plus/Delta		x		x			x				x	
Process Behavior Chart						x			x			
Run Chart						x			x			
Scatter Diagram	x			x	x		x		x			
Visual Synectics				x					x			x
Why-Why					x					x		

Affinity Diagram

What is it?

An Affinity Diagram is a group decision-making technique designed to sort a large number of ideas or opinions into naturally related groups.

Why should I use it?

- Allows for a non-judgmental process for groups to share and categorize ideas
- Gives everyone an opportunity to participate, where all ideas have equal weight

When should I use it?

- To identify and gather large amounts of information, ideas, opinions, or issues, and organize them in a short amount of time
- To surface emerging themes
- To reduce large or complex issues to a manageable size

Examples of use in a library setting

A community-based strategic planning committee organizes brainstorming when creating a library vision.

The technology team identifies the main issues or concerns related to a new automation system before creating a Check Sheet (p. 33).

The staff development committee gathers staff training and development needs and concerns.

The reference department organizes the results of brainstorming, where they generated ideas for improving their services.

Step-by-step instructions

1. State the issue or problem to be explored. Start with a clear statement of the problem or goal.

2. Allow five to ten minutes for each participant to brainstorm ideas (Brainstorming, p. 15) for the issue or problem and to write each idea individually on a sticky note.

3. Participants read ideas and place sticky notes on a flat surface (e.g., desk or wall).

4. Without talking, participants arrange the sticky notes that list related ideas into related groups.

5. Through discussion, continue arranging sticky notes and then create a heading for each grouping that best describes the theme of each group of cards.

Success story

Brownsburg Public Library—a Destination, with and without Walls

Brownsburg Public Library was looking for a way to gather ideas from its customers to include in its strategic plan. The continuous improvement team devised a form. They tried to make the language as open as possible in order to encourage many different kinds of responses. "What is your idea of the PERFECT Library?" the form asked. "Please share your thoughts and ideas with us. We want to know what you think! If money was no object and time wasn't of consideration, my perfect/ideal library would have…." At the bottom were directions to drop off the form at any public service desk or mail it to the library.

The team asked for ideas in a variety of ways. They gathered customer ideas by including the form in the library newsletter, leaving copies on seats at the Volunteer Recognition Night program, circulating forms during a Brownsburg Teen Council meeting, making them available in the library at public service desks and at the library's online catalog stations, and giving them to teachers of ABE (Adult Basic Education) classes held at the library. In addition, they gave forms to staff and board members.

The forms were color-coded so that the library could determine from which audience/group the idea originated.

As the forms began to come back, director Wanda Pearson transferred each idea to a sticky note. (Some forms, of course, contained several ideas and generated several sticky notes.) She added sticky notes to the wall as more forms came in.

During a department head meeting, staff used the Affinity Diagram tool to arrange and categorize the sticky notes. They limited their sorting to a short time period, without talking or discussing the ideas. The staff then discussed their categorization and made some changes.

"During this time we had some interesting discussions about the ideas themselves, especially the more seemingly outlandish ones. For example, one person's 'perfect library' would include an Olympic-sized pool. Even though adding a pool to the library will probably never happen, we discussed where this idea was coming from, or rather, what did it tell us? We realized that the library was used for recreational purposes," noted staff member Kelly Hale. "In addition, we discussed the fact that computers, which were at one time a 'nontraditional' (our subsequent category name) item in libraries, were now a huge part! The Internet has not been around that long either! So we enjoyed looking at the ideas, our past, and seeing how the library is constantly evolving."

After discussing the ideas and coming to a consensus on their grouping, the staff began to see patterns emerging. From these, they named the categories:

Nontraditional Services	Building
Furnishings	Outside
Technology	Patrons
Staff	Materials (Access)
Programs/Services	

"Throughout our discussion and in analyzing the ideas and their subsequent groupings, it appeared that the 'perfect library' was a very real, very physical space in many minds, debunking some naysayers' beliefs that there won't be a need for libraries or a library building, because everything will be available online. On the other hand, technology became a large grouping in our Affinity Diagram, too. Of course, people are very much interested in having as much as possible in the way of computers and software and access to information when they want or need it. The library was a place to meet these needs, too, perhaps an online place, from which people could get information without having to actually walk through the doors," Hale observed. Staff members summarized the results of the diagram and created a draft vision:

> Based on preliminary responses, our library would exist with or without walls, as individuals could choose. The physical facility, combined with programs and services, would evolve into a centralized destination. Materials and staff exist for patrons. However, technology would allow these same individuals to use the library remotely—this same library would encourage use outside its walls. As a result, our resources are provided in response to our patrons' needs and requests. We become a destination—physically and technologically—with and without walls.

When the staff stepped back from the Affinity Diagram, they agreed that the "perfect library" would still meet recreational and physical space needs but would also include lots of technology for information needs. They realized that it was a destination, both physically and remotely. They simplified the vision further and came up with the statement:

> The Brownsburg Public Library becomes a destination—physically and technologically—with and without walls.

At the end of the meeting, the department heads were very pleased with their work and discussions. Director Wanda Pearson reported, "I think it was the best department head meeting we've ever had."

Hints, Cautions, and Tricks

☑ **DO** describe ideas with short phrases or single words.

☑ **DO** remain silent while sorting ideas (sticky notes). The silence forces the participants to pay more attention to the text on the sticky notes.

☑ **DO** discuss ideas while developing the header cards.

☑ **DO** aim for no more than five to ten participants per group. Consider splitting a group if it is much larger than ten.

Agenda

What is it?	An Agenda is a document that helps guide and facilitate a meeting.

Why should I use it?

- Keeps participants focused
- Lets people know the time and location for the meeting
- Keeps track of how many meetings this group has had
- Reminds everyone of the purpose of the meeting
- Establishes the order of the meeting
- Tells who is responsible for portions of the meeting
- Helps evaluate the meeting
- Assists in planning subsequent meetings

When should I use it?

- To run an efficient, productive meeting

Examples of use in a library setting

The library board is meeting.

The staff is holding a committee, team, or all-staff meeting.

A trainer is planning a training session.

Step-by-step instructions

A good agenda has several key elements and looks something like this:

(Comments have been added in italics to clarify the reasons and intent for the elements.)

Agenda
Library Growth Team
7-9 pm, Library Board Room, July 31, 2002
Meeting 8
Keeping track of the number of meetings a group has had reminds everyone of the time they have invested and continuously raises the question of the need to continue and the need to be efficient.

Mission: To develop plans for actively managing growth in both near and long term
It is vital to keep in front of everyone the mission of the group or the purpose for the particular meeting.

Warm-up   All   7:00
Everyone is coming to the meeting from a different situation. Taking a minute or two on a common subject gets everyone focused. Generally ask something as trivial as, "What is your favorite food?" or "What is your favorite color or ice cream flavor?" If the meeting is going to be contentious, see Hints, Cautions, and Tricks (p. 14). If attendance at the meeting is very large, consider leading the group in a few minutes of guided meditation, have the participants do the warm-ups suggested above in small, four- to six-person groups, or use Pair and Share (p. 84).

Agenda Review   All   7:10
Ideally, the agenda for the meeting has been sent to participants prior to the meeting, so the primary purpose of the agenda review is to see if there are items that need to be added to or removed from the agenda, or to reorder the agenda items if desired by those at the meeting.

Subject 1   Jon   7:15
Note that the person who is to lead or report on the agenda item is listed by name. If everyone is to participate, list "All." If there is a lead person but everyone is to participate, list "the person's name/All."

Subject 2   Mari/All   7:30

Generally the biggest problem with meeting agendas is trying to cover too much material in too little time. Unfortunately, there is no solution for this problem other than to guard against trying to pack too much into any meeting. Time estimates help the group manage its time. Some meeting facilitators suggest listing time allowed for each agenda item and appointing a timekeeper to monitor time usage; others find this practice annoying and intrusive.

Assignments   All   7:45

Almost always there is a need to take action as a result of meeting discussion. It is important to summarize what went on in the meeting and establish who has responsibility for what; otherwise, too often nothing gets done between meetings. The person recording minutes is a good person to turn to for the summary. Standard items, like minutes and treasurer's reports, may be handled efficiently by placing them in a "consent" Agenda. Assuming individuals have had an opportunity to review these materials prior to the meeting and they have no comments or questions about the materials, items in the consent Agenda can be dispatched without taking valuable meeting time.

Next meeting date and agenda   All   7:50

These are very important elements of any series of on-going meetings. It is difficult and time-consuming to check everyone's calendar and find a date that everyone is available, so do it at the meeting. Establish the agenda for the next meeting while everyone is together and focused on the purpose of meeting in the first place. The agenda can always be modified, but it is efficient to get the group's consensus on the need for another meeting and, if another meeting is needed, what will be covered.

Meeting evaluation: Plus/Delta (p. 97) All   7:55

13

Success story

Lawrenceburg PL Team Stays on Track

When the Lawrenceburg Public Library District chartered a team to work on improving their process of sending and receiving interlibrary loan materials, team leader Ann Stenger knew she should create an agenda for each meeting. To keep the team focused, she made sure that its mission appeared at the top of each Agenda and that the first order of business was to review the Group Norms (p. 66) that the team had set. She always ended the meeting with a Plus/Delta (p. 97). She added a "to do" list at the bottom of the Agenda, so that each member could make notes of tasks for which he or she had volunteered.

"Having our mission right at the top, reminding ourselves to stick to our meeting norms, and reflecting on what went well in our meeting and what needs improving have really helped our team gain control over their meeting, at the same time that they're improving our delivery process," notes Stenger.

Hints, Cautions, and Tricks

☑ DO keep agendas shorter rather than longer.

☑ DO tailor agendas to meet the needs of the organization. Some agendas need to emphasize reviewing minutes. Some indicate if agenda items are for discussion, information, or decision.

☑ DO consider having the participants do the following if your meeting has very serious overtones or you expect it to be contentious. Choose an object that has some significance to the group—maybe a library coffee mug. Pass the item to the first person and say, "State what is on your mind right now. Be brief and speak from the heart. When you are finished say, 'I'm in' and pass the object to the next person." The next person then does the same until everyone has had a chance to check in. At the end of the meeting, again pass the object and have individuals say, "I'm out." This is a powerful technique and the implication is that: "We are a team. We care about each other, and we are going to contribute positively to the meeting."

☑ DO send the agenda to the participants prior to the meeting.

Brainstorming

What is it?

Brainstorming is a strategy for quickly helping a group generate many solutions without judging or ranking them.

Why should I use it?

- Allows people from different levels and backgrounds to participate equally
- Gathers a wide range of possibilities in a very short time
- Stimulates thinking of each individual through a lively group process
- Discourages focusing on a single solution before examining all the options

When should I use it?

- To solve a problem
- To develop plans
- To generate ideas

Examples of use in a library setting

The library faces a parking problem and needs to find a solution.

The library wants to involve board, staff, and community members in creating a vision for its future.

The library has an opportunity to apply for a foundation grant and needs to generate innovative ideas.

Step-by-step instructions

1. Arrange the furniture so everyone can see and hear.

2. Identify a facilitator, who might be a member of the staff or an outsider. The facilitator has three jobs:

- Keep everyone focused on the task.
- Keep an eye on the clock and help the group finish on time.
- Make sure everyone has a chance to participate.

3. Choose a recorder, who must be able to write fast and to use the participants' words as much as possible, so that the conversation flows without inhibition. The recorder also has three jobs:

- Record every suggestion in the words of the speaker as much as possible.
- Recap comments upon request.
- Notice inconsistencies or incompleteness.

4. If participants don't know each other, ask them to briefly introduce themselves.

5. Prepare participants with a brief explanation of brainstorming and agree upon Group Norms (p. 66) for managing your group:

- Make your brain "itch"; we want lots of ideas.
- Accept all ideas without praise or criticism.
- Speak one at a time.
- Listen carefully.
- Be creative and inventive.
- It's OK to piggyback. Continue to think as you listen to others; if their ideas make you think of others, jot them down.

6. There are as many ways of structuring brainstorming as there are brains; four are offered below with some explanation about the strengths and weaknesses of each. Choose the one that meets your needs and fits with your organizational culture, your work plan, and your time line.

Option 1: Pure Brainstorming

The group focuses its attention on the facilitator and the flip chart or blackboard and shouts out ideas as fast as possible. The recorder (or recorders—you may need more than one to keep up with this fast-paced exercise) adds them to the flip chart. When the page is full, the recorder tears off the sheet and begins on a second page. If there is a lull, the facilitator should not assume that all ideas have been gathered, but should instead wait and encourage the participants to take a moment to review the sheets. Usually they will have another burst of ideas after the pause.

■ Advantages: This is the purest form of brainstorming; it takes advantage of the instant connections that participants make as ideas emerge and doesn't allow time for analysis. It is very lively.
■ Disadvantages: Since the process is designed to be somewhat chaotic, the notes at the end may be hard to disentangle. It is difficult for the facilitator to assure that everyone is participating.

Option 2: Centralized Brainstorming

The group focuses its attention on the facilitator and flip chart or blackboard. Each participant has a few minutes to think and make notes on a piece of paper. The facilitator asks the group to share

one idea at a time, usually by going around the group in an orderly way. As an individual shares an idea, the recorder adds it to the list. If an idea stimulates an additional idea for another person, have that person immediately add the idea to his or her list. Participants are asked to only share ideas that have not yet been mentioned. When the page is full, the recorder tears off the sheet and begins on a second page.

■ Advantages: Centralized brainstorming is fast and is designed to minimize interference in the creative process. It is more orderly than pure brainstorming.
■ Disadvantages: Many ideas are included one after the other on the flip chart pages; sorting and prioritizing them later is more difficult.

Option 3: Sticky Note Brainstorming

This option is similar to centralized brainstorming, where participants have a few minutes to record ideas, but this time they write them on sticky notes. The facilitator must remind them to put only one idea on each sticky note. When everyone has finished writing, the facilitator convenes the group and invites each participant to

share a sticky note and place it on the flip chart or on a wall or other flat surface. If an idea has already been given, the facilitator urges the participant to share another one. The facilitator continues around the group, collecting sticky notes from each participant until they are all gone.

- Advantages: The sticky notes are easy to rearrange when it is time to create an Affinity Diagram (p. 87) or to prioritize options after brainstorming is finished. No recorder is needed.
- Disadvantages: Collecting and adding the sticky notes take longer and cause pauses in the flow of ideas, which may dampen the creative fires or allow participants to analyze and criticize ideas.

Option 4: Structured Brainstorming

The facilitator or the group creates categories to help participants think about different aspects of the issue. Each aspect gets a flip chart page of its own on the wall. The group may break into small

sub-groups to tackle each aspect for a span of time (usually 3-5 minutes), before moving to the next aspect. Alternatively, the group as a whole may visit each aspect. If using small groups, be sure to allow time for each small group to visit each aspect and add their thoughts.

- Advantages: The categories help a group think more deeply about each aspect of the issue. For example, if using brainstorming to create an environmental scan during strategic planning, the categories might include: technology, community initiatives, finances, staffing, services, and facility.
- Disadvantages: The categories are assigned by the facilitator and do not arise naturally from the group.

7. The notes may be organized through an Affinity Diagram (p. 7) for use in the next steps of planning, or prioritized using the Criteria Rating Scale (p. 40), Multivoting (p. 74), Nominal Group Technique (p. 77), or Paired Comparison (p. 87).

Hints, Cautions, and Tricks

☑ DO have a neutral outsider facilitate the brainstorming, if possible, as it is easy for an insider to become engaged in the discussion and forget to record every suggestion, to discourage evaluation, and to make sure everyone gets a chance to speak. If you do use an insider, remember that he or she cannot faciliate *and* contribute ideas.

☑ DO use a warm-up exercise to get the creative juices flowing. Good practice run: Make a list of all the birds you can think of. Divide the audience into groups of four or five people. Give them one minute and have each team make a list. At the end of the time, find out which team has the most birds on their list and read it. If they have "Big Bird" or another fictional bird, look for a negative reaction from other teams which have decided, on their own, not to allow that. Ask, "Did I say they had to be real birds?" Of course, the answer is "No." Use this example to give the teams permission to come up with unusual—even seemingly impossible—ideas.

☑ DO give participants time to think and make notes before beginning the discussion, to level the playing field. Without this preparation time, extroverts will quickly take over the discussion and the group will lose the ideas of the more introverted participants.

☒ DON'T skip Step 5: Norms for Managing Your Group.

☒ DON'T mix brainstorming and analytical thinking. Brainstorming is generative thinking, which is dampened, if not destroyed, by analysis. If you must do both, do the brainstorming first, take a break, and come back for discussion or prioritizing.

Success story

Brainstorming a Vision for the Library

The Dubois County Public Library was creating a strategic plan. The planning committee was made up of two staff members, two board members, and two community members from each of the three library districts in the county—a total of eighteen people—who ranged in age from 17 to 80-something. For their strategic planning, they needed a process for creating a vision for the library. They chose to use Brainstorming Option 3 and to organize the ideas using an Affinity Diagram (p. 7) in the second half of their meeting. The facilitator asked each planning committee member to reflect on the information they had gathered (including trends, customer feedback from focus groups, community and library data), on the service responses that they had selected for the library, and on their knowledge of the community's needs. She encouraged them to think big and be creative. "What would library services look like, feel like, sound like, act like," she asked, "if they were the best they could be, and if time, money, staff, and the facilities were no object?" She gave them each a packet of sticky notes and about 15 minutes to think and write.

When everyone had finished, she began at one side and asked the first person to share one idea. As committee members read their sticky notes, they walked up and stuck them on the wall. The facilitator or someone on the committee occasionally asked a clarifying question, but the facilitator reminded them that this was not the time to evaluate the ideas. Quickly, she went around the room, collecting ideas from each participant. She noticed that a few people were jotting things on new sticky notes and that many were wadding up sticky notes containing ideas already contributed. After a few rounds, most people had run out of ideas, so she asked the remaining few to read all of theirs.

As people walked up and added their sticky notes to the growing collection on the wall, many of them stuck their notes next to others containing a related idea. They were already using their analytical skills to sort ideas into clusters. After a break, they came back and created an Affinity Diagram (p. 7). At the end of the meeting, participants were amazed at how many good ideas the planning committee had generated.

Cause Analysis

What is it?   Cause Analysis is a method to help evaluate which potential causes of an undesirable effect, a failure, or a problem are the best choices to evaluate for improvement.

Why should I use it?
- Reduces the number of possible causes of a problem to a manageable few
- Develops consensus among the team as to which issues are most important to work on and in what order
- Rids the team of feeling overwhelmed with the impossible workload ahead
- Improves the efficiency of a continuous improvement team

When should I use it?
- To decide which potential cause(s) in a Cause-and-Effect Diagram (p. 25) should be worked on for improvement

Examples of use in a library setting

The circulation staff comes up with possible reasons why books are not getting to the shelf in a timely manner.

The facility improvement team identifies possible causes as to why the floors in the library are looking worn after a surprisingly short time.

The library outreach department identifies many reasons why potential bookmobile users don't take advantage of the library's services.

Step-by-step instructions

1. Complete a Cause Analysis worksheet similar to the one below.

 ■ List the causes identified in the Cause-and-Effect Diagram (p. 25).
 ■ Come to consensus on a number scale (e.g., 1-10) that describes how often each cause occurs.
 ■ Come to consensus on a number scale that describes the severity of the individual causes.
 ■ Come to consensus on a number scale that describes how difficult it is to detect the causes when they happen.
 ■ Multiply the three numbers for each cause together and place the product in the Cause Analysis score box.

2. Examine the Cause Analysis scores and decide which potential causes are more likely to generate the results you are experiencing. The causes with the highest scores are good candidates on which to work.

3. Place the results of the worksheet in a Pareto Chart (p. 91) for communication to others.

Success story

Continuous Improvement (CI) Group Examines Possible Causes of Building Complaints

When the Indianapolis CI Libraries group studied patron complaints from participating libraries during one of their sessions, they identified the interior of the building as one of the leading areas of complaints. They decided to use the Cause Analysis chart to help them decide where to work.

First, they listed potential causes of complaints in the left-hand column. Next they arrived at a collective judgment about the frequency, severity, and ease of detection—on a scale of one to ten—for each of the causes.

When they were finished, they were surprised to discover that the leading cause of building complaints—the library being too hot or too cold—might be employees adjusting the thermostat, which certainly was under their own control!

Potential Cause	Frequency Few - - Many 1 - - - - - 10	Severity Low - - High 1 - - - - - 10	Detect-ability Difficult Easy 1 - - - - - 10	Cause Analysis Score (multiply across)
Smelly patrons	2	9	10	180
Custodian issues	2	5	8	80
Water supply	1	7	10	70
Employees adjusting thermostat	8	9	10	720

Hints, Cautions, and Tricks

☑ DO make sure the Cause-and-Effect Diagram from which you are working was done thoughtfully.

☑ DO agree that the potential "cause" you are evaluating is significant and legitimate. Agree on exactly what is meant, i.e., what is the definition of the failure or cause.

☑ DO evaluate what data you already have and/or what data will need to be gathered about individual causes. If no data are available, you may have to go with consensus of the group.

☑ DO agree on whether you are going to do a quick and dirty or an in-depth analysis. Both approaches are legitimate, depending on the situation.

☑ DO have the team come to consensus on how to determine the ratings. Generally this is not difficult and happens naturally. After someone suggests a number, others will chime in and the leader can suggest a number based on what was said. Discussion may follow with consensus being reached following the discussion.

☑ DO remember that the Cause Analysis scores are not etched in stone, and that they must stand the scrutiny of common sense.

☑ DO make sure as many people as possible who have knowledge of the situation are included in the evaluations.

"Fixing the system
is more important
than fixing the blame."
—Phillip C. Schlechty

Cause-and-Effect Diagram

What is it?

The Cause-and-Effect Diagram, also called a fishbone diagram, is used to explore all the potential or real causes that result in a single effect.

Why should I use it?

- Visually displays potential causes of variation
- Generates a substantial list of possible causes in a structured, efficient way

When should I use it?

- To help groups search for root causes
- To identify areas where there may be problems
- To compare the relative importance of different causes
- To encourage everyone to contribute their viewpoints
- To provide a clear illustration of a problem that has been identified by the staff

Examples of use in a library setting

The circulation team studies causes of misshelved items.

Library administrators seek to understand the causes of low morale among the library staff.

A branch library staff seeks to identify the causes of absences.

The children's department staff studies why teenagers are not using the library.

Step-by-step instructions

1. Clearly identify and define the problem or effect.

2. Write the problem in the "effect" box.

3. Draw an arrow that points to the problem.

4. Brainstorm (p. 15) or construct an Affinity Diagram (p. 7) to identify the "major categories" of possible causes. You may summarize causes under standard categories such as:

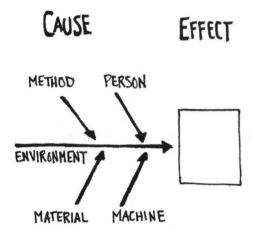

- Machines, Methods, Materials, People, and Environment (This is the preferred option.)
- People, Places, Policies, and Procedures
- People, Policies, and Surroundings
- Suppliers, System, and Skills

5. Draw and label arrows indicating the major categories and point the arrows toward the central arrow.

6. Within each category ask, "What is it about our Methods (Machines, Materials, People, Environment) that may cause this effect?"

7. Continue to add causes to each "bone" until the fishbone is completed.

8. Once all bones have been completed, identify likely, actionable root cause(s) by looking for causes that appear several times or gather data based on hunches and team consensus. (See Cause Analysis, p. 21.)

Hints, Cautions, and Tricks

☑ DO include the people closest to the work; they are most knowledgeable about the process.

☑ DO state causes, not solutions or symptoms.

☑ DO note that the same causes may occur on several bones in the diagram.

☒ DON'T debate or discuss the possible causes as they are initially brainstormed.

Success story

Possible Causes of Building Complaints

Library teams participating in a continuous improvement initiative used complaints received in their libraries over the last few months as the starting point for their Cause-and-Effect Diagram. First they used a Check Sheet (p. 33) to separate complaints into categories. One of the largest categories of complaints was about the library building interior. The teams worked together to identify possible causes of complaints about the interior in each of the five areas on the fishbone:

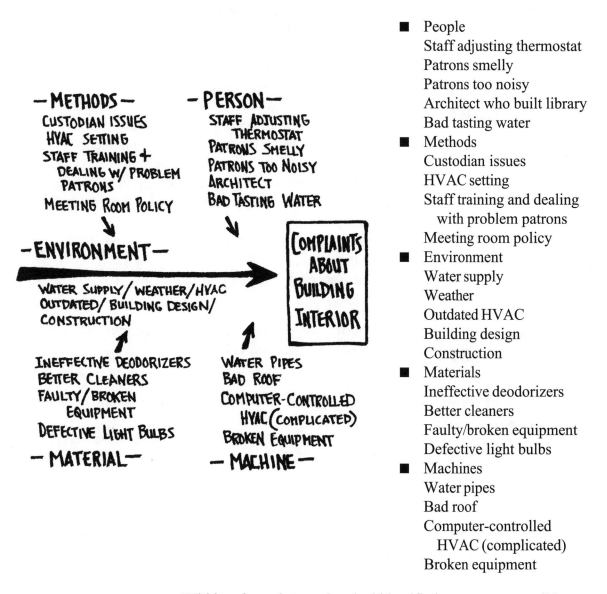

- People
  Staff adjusting thermostat
  Patrons smelly
  Patrons too noisy
  Architect who built library
  Bad tasting water
- Methods
  Custodian issues
  HVAC setting
  Staff training and dealing
    with problem patrons
  Meeting room policy
- Environment
  Water supply
  Weather
  Outdated HVAC
  Building design
  Construction
- Materials
  Ineffective deodorizers
  Better cleaners
  Faulty/broken equipment
  Defective light bulbs
- Machines
  Water pipes
  Bad roof
  Computer-controlled
    HVAC (complicated)
  Broken equipment

Within a few minutes, they had identified twenty-two possible causes.

Charter

What is it?   A Charter is a document written to clearly confer responsibility for accomplishing a task or project on another person or team.

Why should I use it?

- Brings clarity and boundaries to an assignment
- Acts as a contract which must be understood and accepted
- Conveys the seriousness of the assignment
- Establishes a timetable and reporting requirements
- Gives freedom to the person or team to pursue accomplishment of the task or project in any way not limited by the charter
- Ensures that what is asked or expected of a person or team is carefully thought out
- Makes the scope of the project clear to those asked to volunteer
- Ensures accountability and commitment

When should I use it?

- To clarify assignments for task forces, committees, work groups, teams, and individuals.

Examples of use in a library setting

The library organizes a team to install a new computer system.

A department head assigns each staff member an annual goal.

The library administrator asks the adult services department to develop a new outreach program.

The director gives authority to a library-wide task force to improve work attendance.

The community-wide literacy coalition develops a work plan, identifies tasks, and designs task force assignments.

Step-by-step instructions

1. Fill out the charter form in the manner indicated below.

2. Provide a copy to the person or team and agree on its meaning.

DATE: *Issue date*
NUMBER: *For Sequential Tracking*

CHARTER: *List the name*

TO: *Team or person*

FROM: *Sponsor*

PURPOSE: *Describe the purpose or mission of the assignment.*

PRODUCT: *Describe the specific outcomes that are desired.*

AUTHORITY: *Use this area to describe or list authority that is being delegated for carrying out this project.*

LIMITATIONS: *List worries or actions that are unacceptable in carrying out this project. Listing means or actions that are unacceptable frees the person or team to use any other methods or approaches to get the job done.*

MONITORING: *Describe when, how often, in what form, and to whom reports or communication should be made about progress. Many times the phrase, "...or whenever you violate the terms of the charter" is used in this section.*

Below are two examples of charters. The first is a formal, written charter for implementing a new computer system. The second, described in the success story below, is a more informal approach, which yielded quick and effective results for a small library wishing to improve its shelving process.

	DATE: July 17, 2000
	NUMBER: 1-00

CHARTER: New Computer System

TO: Steve Pesek

FROM: Ray Wilson

PURPOSE: To get the new computer system up and running

PRODUCT: The system will be installed and tailored to our method of doing business. All employees will be trained in use of the computer.

AUTHORITY: To work with suppliers, buyers, and IS personnel as necessary. To spend up to $100,000.

LIMITATIONS: Do not fail to:
    Keep change orders to a minimum (Maximum cost $10,000)
    Involve all supervisors in the review and design of the system
    Plan for full integration into the accounting system in the future
    Meet the start-up date of September 1
    Inform me if we are getting behind schedule

MONITORING: Monthly written report
    Quarterly verbal briefing

Hints, Cautions, and Tricks

☑ DO establish who has the right and responsibility to write charters. These same people should probably be responsible for monitoring progress.

☑ DO be precise and clear in the words used in the charter.

☑ DO make sure that the person or team accepting the charter understands what is expected and that all of their questions are answered.

☑ DO be sure that all of the worries of the person or group writing the charter are covered in the Limitations section of the charter.

☑ DO adjust the headings in the charter to meet your needs and culture. Some people are offended by such words as "Authority" and "Monitoring." If this is the case simply substitute other words with the same meaning such as "Permissions" and "Reporting."

Success story

Lawrenceburg Solves Shelving Problems

Complaints about shelving had been increasing from members of the circulation staff and from their manager. After the library decided to discontinue hiring student pages and asked every member of the circulation staff to assist with shelving throughout the day, some staff felt they were doing more than their share. More and more often, circulation manager Debra Beckett reported that she noticed carts full of unshelved books near the end of the day and had to remind the staff to take care of them. She and Sally Stegner, Director of the Lawrenceburg Public Library, decided to take action.

They set up a meeting with the circulation staff and gave them a task: to improve the shelving process. The staff would have 30 minutes, without the circulation manager or director present, to come up with a proposed solution. She requested that the staff propose a way to test the new process and make a report on their progress at the end of the half-hour meeting. The solution would have to:

- ■ Assure timely and accurate shelving
- ■ Share the task equitably among the circulation staff
- ■ Require no intervention by the department head
- ■ Require no new staff

In half an hour, the staff came up with a workable solution. On each shift, one of the two staff members would be assigned to handle information and the other would handle circulation. The two would work out between them who would shelve what types of materials. They would check the book drop every hour, reminded by the clock in the children's room that chimes every hour. The staff agreed on a way to sort the materials on the cart in advance of shelving: fiction on the left, non-fiction on the right, media on the second shelf. They decided to try the process for six weeks and then reconvene to discuss whether it was working.

When they reported their results, both Stegner and Beckett were well pleased. The proposal met all their requirements and seemed simple to implement. The circulation staff sent a memo to other staff members to share the new process.

The circulation staff now "own" the process and they have agreed to help each other remember to implement it. One staff member commented, "I never meant to [neglect shelving]. I would just get involved in other things and run out of time. I appreciate it when someone reminds me, because I know it's important."

A few weeks into the six-week test period, Stegner observed, "The new shelving process seems to be working. We're happy with the results of our first attempt to charter a team. We have been coming up with many ideas of areas we can improve. We are excited about it."

Check Sheet

What is it?

A Check Sheet is simply a record, often described as "hash marks," of the number of occurrences of an action or event. It is generally a good tool to use at the beginning of any problem-solving cycle.

Why should I use it?

- Quickly records activity or transaction, manually or through automated recording

When should I use it?

- To keep track of occurrences over a period of time, from various staff members, or at various locations
- To begin to detect patterns

Examples of use in a library setting

The library tracks circulation—via its automated system—by location, by hour, by day, and by collection category.

The circulation staff keeps track of problems that result in materials being misshelved.

The library subscribes to a service that counts web site hits.

Step-by-step instructions

1. Using data on problems or occurrences encountered in the recent past, design a manual or automated system for recording occurrences of the events you wish to study.

2. Work with the staff and the software vendor, if necessary, to create shared Operational Definitions (p. 81) of each event.

3. Train staff in use of the Check Sheet, supported by the Operational Definition (p. 81).

4. Gather data. Decide over what period of time the data will be gathered—one data sheet per day or month, etc.

Success story
  Bloomfield Surveys Teens

Karen Holz, Eastern Branch Librarian, and the rest of the staff at the Bloomfield-Eastern Greene County Public Library knew that use among teenagers was low. They wanted to find out why and what they could do to increase useage. The staff designed a survey that would take about five minutes to complete. They worked with English teachers at the high schools in Bloomfield and Eastern to have students fill it out during class. On the survey, the library included the following questions:

Are you male/female?
Which high school do you attend?
Do you use the library?
If yes, how often?
  Once a week
  Once a month
  Once a year
If yes, for what purposes?
  Entertainment reading
  Class assignment
  Internet
  Meet friends
  Other:
If no, why not?
  No time
  Didn't know there was one
  Don't know what's there
  Don't feel comfortable with the facility
  Staff
  Don't have transportation
  Don't have a library card
  Don't read
  Other:

When all the surveys had been returned to the library, the staff created a database, "an automated Check Sheet," as Holz described it, to compile the data. She was able to quickly enter the data from each survey, then tally the total number of surveys, and disaggregate the data by gender, by high school, and by frequency of use. She could use the data to create Pareto Charts (p. 91) showing which purposes accounted for the most uses and which reasons kept teenagers from using the library.

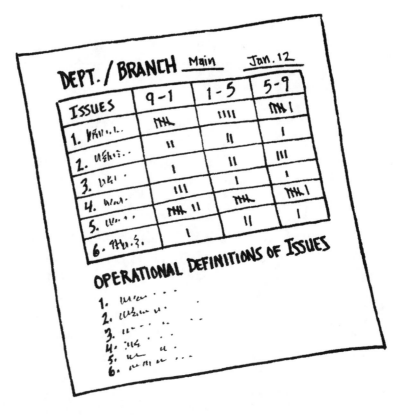

She found that students at both high schools made heaviest use of recreational reading, followed by information for class assignments. At Eastern, the biggest reasons for non-use were lack of time and transportation. At Bloomfield, staff issues cropped up on the survey. The library is planning some professional development for staff about developmental needs of teens, is continuing to add new recreational reading materials, and is working on figuring out how to address the time and transportation issues. "We may have to take the library to where the kids are," she mused. Meanwhile, circulation over the summer, since the survey, has soared. "We don't know why for sure," she noted, "but we suspect it's related to the really great high school page we had. She attracted lots of her friends and was a great role model of library use."

Hints, Cautions, and Tricks

☑ DO design the categories for data so the Check Sheet will yield useful detail. For example, if the library wants to study its reference process, it may want to look at the data to determine which days, hours, and locations are busier or less busy, so the Check Sheet should be laid out to identify location (different service points in a single building or different branches), date, and hours, as shown in the illustration.

☑ DO arrive at a commonly understood Operational Definition (p. 81) for each category to reduce variation in counting. For example, a "ready reference question" might be defined as "a phone or walk-in question where the staff uses a resource at the reference desk and takes 30 seconds or less to find the answer."

☑ DO find a way to help staff remember to add a check for each transaction. There is a natural tendency to get busy and forget to add hash marks and then to compensate by adding a batch when traffic slows. Encourage staff to make the Check Sheet as accurate as possible.

☑ DO assure staff that the data will be used to understand the system, not to evaluate their performance.

☑ DO be sure you understand the data that are being recorded. For example, web hits included in a report may reflect staff use as well as customer use of the web site or may be overstated on days when web pages are modified. Hits may indicate poor design rather than heavy use, if, for example, users are forced to backtrack to the home page at every step of their search.

☑ DO realize that hand-written descriptions of occurrences may need to be done for a few periods/days just to get a sense of what the general categories should be that will be listed on the Check Sheet. It is not uncommon to have "Other" category that covers miscellaneous occurrences that don't fit elsewhere.

Consensogram

What is it?
A survey used to measure a group's current knowledge or perception of an issue.

Why should I use it?
- Displays results quickly and allows individuals to see their responses in relationship to the group

When should I use it?
- To display data from an entire group, not just a few individuals
- To determine the frequency of distribution of responses
- To determine a group's current knowledge about an issue or agreement with a course of action

Examples of use in a library setting
The continuous improvement team starts a discussion at a library staff meeting on the percentage of staff time wasted.

Workshop presenters assess how much participants know about a topic before and after training.

The library's technology implementation task force determines how prepared the staff is for migrating to a new automation system.

The library's consultant checks the community planning committee's level of agreement with the proposed strategic plan.

Step-by-step instructions
1. State and write the issue or question to be measured.

2. Draw X and Y axes as the beginnings of a frequency chart. Put tick marks along the Y axis going from 0 to 100 percent.

3.   Give each person a sticky note.

4.   Ask the question, e.g., "How ready are we to install the new automation system?" and invite each individual to answer that question by writing a number, in increments of 10 percent, on their sticky note.

5.   Place the individual sticky notes above the corresponding number on the frequency chart.

6.   Encourage group observations about results.

Success story

Staff Shows Their Support for Library Values

The staff and five board members of the Kendallville library spent a day working on developing their library's Constancy of Purpose Statement (mission, vision, values, and measures), with facilitator Ray Wilson.

At the conclusion of drafting the library's values, Wilson gave participants each a 3" x 5" sticky note and asked them to express their satisfaction with the values that they had just developed. They were asked to do this by placing a number, in 10 percent increments between 0 and 100 percent, on their sticky notes. Zero represented total dissatisfaction and 100 meant total satisfaction.   They were then asked to place their sticky notes on the flip chart graph that had been prepared. When they were finished, the results looked like the illustration:

Next the group developed its mission statement. When they were finished, they again did a consensogram to see how the group felt about it.

After each consensogram vote, the group acknowledged that they realized that the documents they had just developed were drafts and that they might need

to tweak them a bit. They also said that, as they live with them and as the documents develop their full meaning, they expected that more individuals would vote 100 percent acceptance and satisfaction.

Library Director Jenny Draper posted the draft mission, vision, and values, along with the consensograms, in the staff lounge and invited the staff to think about and discuss them. Over a period of three weeks, the sticky notes moved up, until almost all were at 90 percent or higher.

"I think the staff needed time to think about our mission, vision, and values," she concluded. "Now I know they feel very comfortable with all three."

Hints, Cautions, and Tricks

☑ DO keep responses anonymous. Having the facilitator place the sticky notes on the frequency chart can provide even more anonymity.

☑ DO test critical issues frequently.

☑ DO be prepared to act on the data results.

☑ DO be prepared when some participants write a number that is not an even 10 percent increment. Simply place it near its proper location.

☒ DON'T discuss responses until all data have been posted.

"Trust is an important
lubricant of a social system.
It is extremely efficient;
it saves a lot of trouble
to have a fair degree of reliance
on other peoples' word."
—*Kenneth Arrow*

Criteria Rating Scale

What is it?
Criteria Rating is a data-based decision-making strategy.

Why should I use it?
- Provides objective criteria to compare data that helps a team reach agreement
- Presents results graphically and easily

When should I use it?
- To make any decision in which a number of factors must be considered

Examples of use in a library setting

A selection committee identifies criteria for hiring or promotion, prioritizes them, and ranks candidates according to the criteria.

The technology team uses specifications for a new automated system to rate vendor responses.

Working with school reading specialists, children's staff identifies criteria for choosing a reading program and ranks each program against the criteria.

After being offered a new position, an individual staff member creates criteria and ranks the options to decide whether to accept the offer or not.

"The only reason to gather data is to take action."
—William Scherkenbach

Step-by-step instructions

1. Determine and list the criteria that you will use to make the selection in the left-hand column. For example, in hiring a new staff member for the children's department, the criteria on your list might include the knowledge, skills, and abilities listed in the job description. See page 43 for a completed example.

2. Scale each criterion on a scale of 1 to 5. Scale the criteria so that a "5" is always the most-desired state and "1" is the least-desired state. For example, more years of experience would be more desirable, so the scale might run from 0-1 years for 1 point, 2-3 years for 2 points, etc. On the other hand, more criminal convictions would be undesirable, so a "5" there would indicate no convictions, while a "1" would be correlated with two or more convictions.

3. In the "Weighting" column, give each criterion a weight. Use 0, .5, 1.0, 1.5, and 2.0. In the staff hiring example, for instance, you might weight education heaviest, giving it a 2.0, and experience with Spanish-language selection as a .5, important but not essential.

4. Across the top, list the options or alternatives that are to be evaluated. In our example on page 43, the candidates' names are listed across the top.

CRITERIA RATING FORM

CRITERIA	WEIGHTING	OPTION 1	OPTION 2	OPTION 3	OPTION 4
1 2 3 4 5					
1 2 3 4 5					
1 2 3 4 5					
1 2 3 4 5					
TOTAL					

5. Rate the performance of each option for every criterion. In our example, John's resume shows that he has an MLS, has worked on the reference desk in a library for nine years, has taken a course in early childhood development, and has been on the library's web site development team. He indicated in the interview that he does not speak Spanish. A call to the police department confirms that he has no record of convictions.

6. Multiply the performance rating by the criteria weights and add the products across each alternative. If, for example, John has an MLS and qualifies for a "5" rating and the committee has weighted education at 2.0, you would multiply 5 by 2.0 and give John a "10" in that cell.

7. Total the columns to yield an overall rating for each option. If one candidate is clearly superior, you may not need much discussion beyond this point. If there is a tie, or if two candidates are close, you may need to continue the discussion, have a second interview, or check additional references until the selection committee reaches consensus.

Hints, Cautions, and Tricks

☑ DO remember that the criteria are subjective, as are the weights assigned each one, so the validity of the criteria rating process will only be useful if the group agrees on criteria and weights and rates them in good faith.

☑ DO use Criteria Rating to reduce the number of choices or to allow factors to surface for further discussion. Results of criteria rating provide a focus for discussion, rather than a final decision.

☒ DON'T forget to create Group Norms (p. 66).

Children's Librarian Opening					
Criteria	**Weight**	**Option 1** Hector	**Option 2** John	**Option 3** Tawanda	**Option 4** Steve
Education 5 = MLS; 4 = B.S./B.A; 3 = Some college; 2 = HS Grad; 1 = Some HS	2.0	10.0	8.0	6.0	6.0
Library Experience 5 = 8 yrs +; 4 = 6-7 yrs; 3 = 4-5 yrs; 2 = 2-3 yrs; 1 = 0-1 yrs.	1.5	7.5	6.0	4.5	3.0
Knowledge of Child Development 5 = Substantive; 1 = None	1.0	3.0	5.0	1.0	1.0
Customer Service Experience 5 = Substantive; 1 = None	1.5	7.5	6.0	7.5	3.0
Computer Skills 5 = Substantive; 1 = None	1.0	5.0	5.0	5.0	5.0
Proficiency with Spanish 5 = Fluent; 1 = None	.5	.5	1.5	2.5	2.5
Criminal Convictions 5 = None; 1 = 1 or more	2.0	10.0	2.0	10.0	10.0
Total		43.5	33.5	36.5	30.5

Success story

Kendallville Chooses a New Automation System

The Kendallville Public Library needed a new automation system. They invited three vendors to make presentations to the whole staff at the library and had completed the first presentation when Director Jenny Draper discovered the Criteria Rating tool. She and the six department heads met and together they listed criteria and weighted them. "We didn't have a Request for

Proposal (RFP), but we decided on the criteria from working with our customers and our existing system," she said. "With all the department heads contributing, we had a pretty complete picture of what we needed the system to do."

Criteria and their weights were:

Support	2.0
User friendly	2.0
Weeding	1.5
Reserves/Status/Building	1.5
Inquiry	1.5
Statistical Reports	1.5
Item History	1.5
OPAC/Web	1.5
Label Program	1.0
Status New Books	1.0
Acquisitions	1.0
Pay-All Easily	1.0
Children's Search	0.5
Loan History	0.5
Choice on Receipt/Easily	0.5

They gave the form to all full-time and part-time staff before the remaining two presentations and asked them to complete one for the previous presentation and one after each of the other two. When all the forms were collected, a clear winner emerged.

Accounting for the fact that she introduced the form in the middle of the presentations, Draper wondered if the first presentation might have ranked higher if the staff had had the Criteria Rating form to use, but she recognized its value and didn't regret inserting it.

"I was glad to find the Criteria Rating tool," she noted. "It was easy for us to come up with the criteria. Using this, everyone was looking for the same things. It made an impact on the questions our staff asked. I could have waited to use it, but I realized we didn't have a good process in place for making this important decision. Without some agreed-upon criteria, staff members would vote for one automation system or another and I wouldn't know why. I wouldn't have a good basis for comparison. I'll use Criteria Rating again."

Fishbowl

What is it?

Fishbowl is a technique that allows one group to demonstrate a technique, while another observes and gives feedback.

Why should I use it?

- Reveals many levels of group behavior by allowing group members to alternately watch and participate in an activity
- Keeps all members of a group engaged in learning when the activity allows only a small group to participate actively
- Encourages timid or resistant members of a group to take part in an activity

When should I use it?

- During training, to provide a non-threatening way for members of a group who are reticent to try a new procedure
- To encourage those who are reticent to speak out in all-staff meetings
- To help group members understand the importance of context and strategy, as well as the content of discussion

Examples of use in a library setting

As part of the reference interview training for new employees, seasoned staff members demonstrate the library's reference interview process while the new employees observe and give feedback. Later, the new employees try the process and receive feedback from the seasoned staff.

Staff of one library department has been reading a book together and discussing it as a group. They use the fishbowl technique to demonstrate to skeptical staff from other departments how it works.

Step-by-step instructions

1. Choose a group to participate and another to watch.

2. The participants perform the task. Usually the participants will choose a facilitator and perhaps a recorder. This group speaks freely, following the Group Norms (p. 66) they have set with the facilitator, as they complete the task at hand.

3. The watchers watch silently as the participants complete their work. The watchers may be expected to look for certain behaviors or to follow guidelines, take notes, or otherwise record their observations. They do not talk to each other or contribute to the participants' conversation.

4. After the participants have completed the task, the two groups share their observations, which will usually include comments on the content, comments on the procedure, and comments on the context within which the participants' discussion took place.

The groups may switch positions for a second fishbowl, with participants becoming watchers and vice versa.

Hints, Cautions, and Tricks

☑ DO keep the participating group to no larger than six or eight people, so that each person gets a chance to speak. The observer group may be larger.

☑ DO keep the exercise short and provide an observation framework, so that the attention of observers doesn't wander.

☑ DO consider physical arrangements so that observers can see and hear without intruding on the fishbowl participants.

☑ DO create guidelines for productive discussion so that observer comments do not become personal.

Success story

How Do You Shelve?

The Brownsburg Public Library had identified a key process: shelving adult fiction books in an accurate and timely manner. The staff needed to look at the workflow of shelving from the pages' point of view. They realized that they had to listen to the pages. The Fishbowl approach proved to be an effective and simple way to facilitate clear communication.

Eight of the library's ten pages are high school students who work during the evenings and weekends. The staff wanted to include them on a process mastering team, but that was logistically impossible, so, prior to the beginning of the school year, they scheduled a meeting for both the pages and members of the continuous improvement (CI) team. Staff facilitator Ardith Peterson let the CI team members know that they were to listen and learn on the outside of the Fishbowl. The pages knew that others would attend and that the agenda was to discuss shelving.

"Writing about shelving is as dull as dirt," observed Peterson. "Talking about it was a little more interesting. I posed the question, 'How do you shelve?'"

The members of the Fishbowl and observers quickly learned that one standard wasn't applied to all collections. According to the pages, all adult non-fiction is in absolute order and adult fiction is put in order by author and then title, but in the junior department, all bets were off. There were several variations that worked well in juniors but varied from the expectations in adult fiction and non-fiction. It clearly illustrated to everyone listening that they had to subdivide the library's shelving into processes. The CI team had initially thought that they could choose "Shelving accurately" as a process. Absolutely not possible! There were too many variations.

The discussion remained focused on how items are shelved. It seemed that the pages doing the work knew what the standard was in the adult fiction area. The problem was that the materials were not accurately shelved. A few days prior to the meeting, the facilitator had randomly selected five books to be shelved in each of the library's three areas—junior, adult fiction and adult non-fiction. She had checked the shelves to see if they were shelved according to the library's standard of absolute Dewey order in adult non-fiction and author/title order in adult fiction. She also applied the same standard in Junior. Results: None of the five adult fiction books were correctly shelved; three of five adult non-fiction and one of five junior titles were correct.

The pages talked about overcrowded shelves, spine labels that were very difficult to read, labeling on shelves that was not helpful, and too few extra shelves for shifting books as needed. The CI team learned that their messages about accuracy included all kinds of variation.

After the Fishbowl, the CI team knew that they had three shelving processes—adult fiction, adult non-fiction, and junior—and that each would have to have a separate process master. They had learned about some of the causes of shelving problems.

"Incidentally," reports Peterson, "we have plotted points and when we last checked, adult fiction was 80 percent accurate. That's progress!"

*"What we call little things
are merely the causes of great things;
they are the beginning, the embryo,
and it is the point of departure which,
generally speaking,
decides the whole future of an existence."
—Henri Frederic Amiel*

Flowchart: Deployment

What is it?

A Deployment Flowchart is a visual representation of all the steps in a process displayed in a manner that indicates who is responsible for the steps and in what order they are accomplished.

Why should I use it?

- Brings clarity and agreement on who is responsible for tasks in a single process
- Provides a foundation for improvement
- Improves efficiency in planning new processes or projects
- Gives everyone a simple picture of the overall process and the interrelatedness of the individual steps

When should I use it?

- To convey a schematic picture of who is responsible for various tasks in a process
- To plan the steps in a new or proposed process or project
- To look for unnecessary steps in a process
- To communicate where problems occur and to study ways to improve a process
- To help train new employees

Examples of use in a library setting

A librarian plans a children's summer reading program which includes many staff members at several locations.

A staff member arranges tours of the library.

The Board plans a building project and wants to define the responsibilities of the Board, staff, library construction manager, and contractor.

The Director puts together a budget and wants to ensure that customers, departments, and Board members have input and that the budget meets legal timetables.

The library develops a proposal for foundation funding involving several departments in the library as well as community partners.

Step-by-step instructions

1. Decide on a name and beginning and ending points (the boundary) for the process.

2. Write the cast of characters (position titles) who are involved in the process on 3" x 5" sticky notes and place them across the top of a flip chart page or on a wall.

3. Write the first step in the process on a sticky note and place it under the character who is responsible for doing it.

4. Continue by writing the second and subsequent steps on sticky notes and placing them in descending order under the characters who will accomplish those steps.

5. When all steps are listed and everyone is satisfied with them and their order, number the steps. Place 1, 2, 3, etc., on each of the sticky notes.

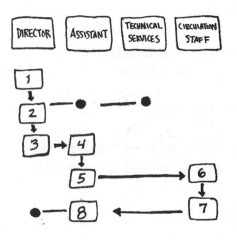

6. Once the team agrees upon the order and assignment of tasks, add arrows to show the flow of work and dots with lines to indicate "supporting characters."

50

Hints, Cautions, and Tricks

☑ DO insist on every step beginning with an action verb.

☑ DO use 3" x 5" sticky notes when constructing the flowchart. This makes it easy to make changes.

☑ DO give a name to the process you are flowcharting. This may be more difficult than it first appears, but it is very helpful in defining the beginning and ending points of the process. Don't be surprised if you need to change the beginning or ending point of the process as you flowchart.

☑ DO decide at what level of detail to flowchart, as the team begins listing steps in the process. Depending on the complexity of the process and the objective of doing the flowchart, the team will need to decide on what level of detail to include. Initially, it is generally best to work at a higher (less detailed) level.

☑ DO recognize that members of the team developing the flowchart will have different ideas about the steps and their order. Ultimately they will need to agree on one "flow" for the process.

☑ DO resist the temptation, for existing processes, to flowchart the process as it should be. Stick to flowcharting the process as it is.

☑ DO limit processes to fifty or fewer steps. Although flowcharts can have any number of steps or tasks, it is generally recommended that teams choose narrower rather than wider boundaries.

☑ DO list the cast of characters by position title rather than by individual's name. Although there is no correct way to position the characters across the top of the flip chart page, sometimes it is helpful to arrange them in a manner that keeps connecting arrows from making too many crossovers.

☑ DO have the team identify the suppliers, customers, inputs, and outputs for their process as a learning bonus while developing the flowchart.

☒ DON'T draw arrows between sticky notes until you are fairly certain you have all the steps included and in the right position.

Success story

Wells County Deploys Staff to Accomplish Plan

Director Stephanie Davis and the staff of the Wells County Public Library were completing a strategic plan. With their facilitator and community planning committee, they had conducted focus groups, analyzed data, and decided on a course of action. They felt the plan was important and workable and they didn't want it to sit on the shelf.

"We want to be such a vital, important place in the community that, five years from now, when we go to the public with a plan to add on to our building, they'll say, 'Surely, of course,'" added Teresa Dustman, Assistant Children's Librarian.

To map out who would be responsible for implementing the plan, the staff worked together to plot every objective on a Deployment Flowchart. "We knew that the plan would involve the whole staff," notes Davis, "so we weren't surprised to see how many people were involved, but this made us realize that it was 'top-heavy' in two ways. First, in the plan, we had proposed to start on everything right away. It is so hard not to begin immediately, once you've identified the needs, but we could see from the flowchart that we had to spread things out over a couple of years. Second, we realized that many of the actions depended on me to initiate them—either to find funding or start a new service. I was feeling the burden of that responsibility, but now I can see from the flowchart that at least after the service, funding, and people are in place, I can turn them over to other staff members to continue. The department heads will actually have most of the responsibility, but the plan is spread over all the departments, dividing the work among many people. We are counting on this flowchart, along with our Gantt Chart (p. 63), to keep us focused and on schedule. In the end the plan will mean more to the staff since they will have such an investment in it."

In their Deployment Flowchart (part of which is reproduced on the following page), the Wells County Public Library staff used a numbering system that refers to the goals, objectives, and actions in their strategic plan, so, for example, 1.1.1c, the first box under "Department Heads," is Action 1c under Goal 1, Objective 1.

Goal 1 is:

WCPL provides an attractive, safe, and valued community destination where county residents gather to learn, exchange information, socialize, and enjoy themselves.

Objective 1 is:

Throughout this planning cycle, increase public awareness in certain identified areas as measured by usage, program attendance, and survey results.

Using this method, the Board and director can see clearly that each action has been assigned. Staff members can see what they and their departments will be working on and how it fits into the Library's overall plan.

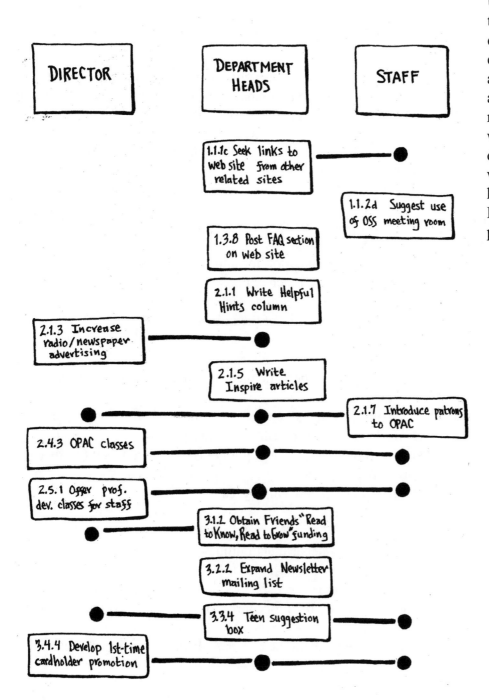

Flowchart: Top-Down

What is it?

A Top-Down Flowchart is a visual representation of all the steps in a process* segregated into major steps and sub-steps, placed in the order in which they are accomplished.

*A process is a grouping in sequence of all interrelated tasks directed at producing one particular outcome.

Why should I use it?

- Brings clarity to and agreement on the logical steps in a process
- Provides a foundation for improvement
- Improves the efficiency in planning new processes or projects
- Gives everyone a simple picture of the overall process and the interrelatedness of the individual steps

When should I use it?

- To convey a schematic picture of the order of tasks within a process
- To plan the steps in a new or proposed process or project
- To look for unnecessary steps in a process
- To communicate where problems occur and to study ways to improve a process
- To help train new employees

Examples of use in a library setting

The purchasing department outlines tasks involved in ordering books.

Librarians clarify the procedures for repairing books or videos.

Custodians document the tasks involved in cleaning the restrooms.

A staff team lists steps in shelving books.

The Director orders the tasks necessary for planning a board meeting.

The accounting department identifies the procedures involved in paying invoices.

Step-by-step instructions

1. Decide on a name and beginning and ending points (the boundary) for the process.

2. Write the major or general steps in the process on 3' x 5" sticky notes and place them in sequential order across the top of a flip chart page or on a wall.

3. After there is reasonable satisfaction with the listing and layout of the major steps, begin developing the sub-steps under the first major step. Write sub-steps or tasks on sticky notes and place them in order of occurrence under the first major step.

4. Continue developing the flowchart by repeating Step 3 for subsequent major steps. Move the sticky notes as you discuss the steps and their logical order.

5. When all steps are listed and everyone is satisfied with them and their order, number the steps. Place 1.0, 2.0, 3.0, etc., on each of the major step sticky notes. Write 1.1, 1.2, 1.3, etc., on the sub-steps under the first major step. Do the same, 2.1, 2.2, 2.3, etc., for the remaining sub-steps.

Hints, Cautions, and Tricks

☑ DO insist on every step beginning with an action verb.

☑ DO use 3" x 5" sticky notes when constructing the flowchart. This reduces the temptation to not make changes that will require major revisions.

☑ DO give a name to the process you are flowcharting. This may be more difficult than it first appears, but it is very helpful in defining the beginning and ending points of the process. Don't be surprised if you need to change the beginning or ending point of the process as you flowchart.

☑ DO decide the level of detail at which to work. As the team begins listing steps in the process, either consciously or unconsciously, it will need to decide on what level of detail to include in the flowchart. This will depend on the complexity of the process and the objective of doing the flowchart. It is generally best to work at a higher (less detailed) level initially.

☑ DO be flexible. Even though you begin by asking for the major steps in the process, be prepared to acknowledge that many steps initially considered major will be discarded or moved to sub-step locations.

☑ DO recognize that members of the team developing the flowchart will have different ideas about the steps and their order. Ultimately they will need to agree on <u>one</u> "flow" for the process.

☑ DO resist the temptation to flowchart the process <u>as it should be</u>. Stick to flowcharting the process <u>as it is</u>.

☑ DO encourage the team to limit processes to fifty or fewer steps. It is also desirable to limit the number of major steps to six to nine and the number of sub-steps per major step to five to seven. These are just rules of thumb, but if your flowchart differs significantly you may want to consider rearranging or setting different boundaries.

☑ DO have the team identify the suppliers, customers, inputs, and outputs for their process, as a learning bonus while developing the flowchart.

Success story

Peabody Takes a Look at Check-in of Returned Materials

Ray Ranier, Head of Adult Services at Peabody Public Library, read *Process Mastering* by Ray Wilson just before a staff meeting. At the meeting, he asked the staff to help him make a list of all the processes in the library. The list covered three pages. They decided to make their first process master on the materials return process, since it was the "biggest can of worms."

"We have long recognized the problems associated with the check-in of returned materials at our library. Moving between two floors and several staff members, mistakes were common, due to lack of regimentation and uniformity of the process. We asked the staffers involved in the various stages of the process (collecting returned items, scanning, reactivating, etc.) for their input. These ideas were then grouped together using an Affinity Diagram (p. 7) into five main processes seen across the top of the Flowchart."

With help from all the departments, the Adult Services staff drafted a Top-Down Flowchart. "We realized they were all involved in getting the materials back on the shelves," noted Ray. They shared the basic flowchart with the rest of the staff and got their input. "We really don't do it like this," some said. Others added, "Actually, we have this other step in here."

The chart was adjusted according to these suggestions and returned for further comment. Once the flowchart was finalized, it was given to our head of circulation, who created specific flowchart procedures for the processes.

Peabody staff check in materials differently now. They eliminated a check-in verification step. Instead of taking carts of materials downstairs to the Technical Services area for check-in, they handle check-in right in the Circulation workroom. "We didn't have to shift staff. We took work away from the pages when we eliminated the verification step."

Ranier has been plotting numbers of "claims returned" books found on the shelves. The mistakes have reduced dramatically.

"We were just thinking the other day. We're going to get heavily into turning out process masters. It's really helping us serve our customers better."

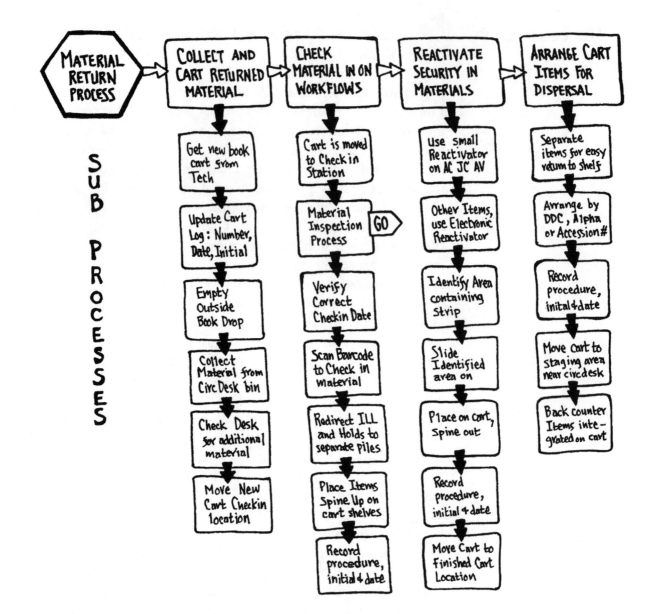

Note that the arrow with the word "GO" attached to one of the steps in the flowchart indicates that there is an additional process to consult for more detail.

*"As you can imagine,
every organization is comprised
of hundreds—even thousands—
of interlocking processes."
—Diane Galloway*

Force Field

What is it?
A Force Field diagram is a visual representation of the struggle between the forces that are pushing for change and those that are resisting change.

Why should I use it?
- Helps a team visualize what issues they are up against
- Provides a list of potential starting points from which to take action
- Encourages creative thinking
- Allows a team to build consensus on what they can effect and what they can't

When should I use it?
- To get a group's perspective on what is driving and what is preventing something from happening
- To brainstorm ideas about how to get started on a change
- To get moving when a team is stuck
- To overcome the inertia resulting from the unknown

Examples of use in a library setting
The board and staff are embarking on transformational continuous improvement in the library.

The library board is planning for a community campaign to raise funds for an addition to the existing library and needs to identify possible hurdles.

The library is considering a new information technology system, but opinions of department heads differ on whether a new system is needed and, if so, which features should be added.

The library needs to improve cost-effectiveness, but some staff members feel that they are being accused of being inefficient or lazy.

Step-by-step instructions

1. Begin by writing the general issue at the top of a flip chart page. Below that, draw a horizontal line across the page and a vertical line down the middle of the page. Above the horizontal line, on the left, write: "Forces Driving [the change]" and on the right "Forces Restraining [the change]."

2. Ask each person to take five minutes and write down all the Driving Forces. Follow that with five minutes to list all the Restraining Forces.

3. Consolidate everyone's ideas onto a master list on the flip chart page. List forces only once.

4. Discuss the results as a group. It is more valuable to remove Restraining Forces than it is to enhance Driving Forces.

5. Decide which Restraining Forces you as a group can affect.

6. Prioritize the order in which you will tackle the Restraining Forces. Multivoting (p. 74) or Nominal Group Technique (p. 77) is helpful for this.

7. Charter a person or team(s) to begin the work (p. 28).

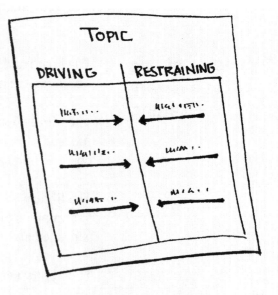

Success story

Teens in a Force Field

Many participants in the Indiana Continuous Improvement Initiative identified "attracting teens to the library" as one of their key success factors. They tried out the Force Field analysis tool on this challenge.

"What is driving teens to come to the library?" they asked. They used brainstorming to create a list of driving forces:

> Homework
> Place to hang out
> Rewards and incentives
> Computers
> Information
> Free printer paper
> Like the library
> Social place
> CDs and music
> Building a resume
> Credit for community service

Next they identified what forces were restraining teens from coming to the library:

> Lack of transportation
> Extracurricular activities
> Uncool image
> Lack of time
> Previous bad experiences
> Can't use computers
> No special space
> Unwelcome
> Hours not late enough
> No food or drink
> Don't know how to use
> Treated badly

Within a few minutes, they had created a substantial list of driving and restraining forces. When they studied the restraints, they realized that they could directly or indirectly address every item on the list. Next, they used Multivoting (p. 74) to prioritize the most important restraints.

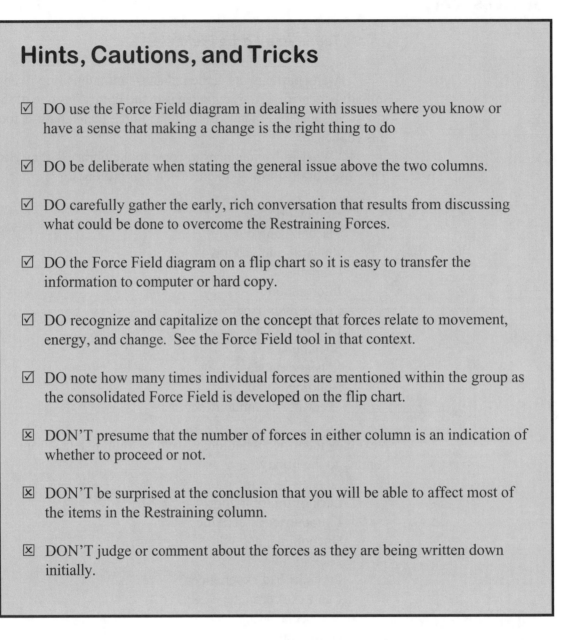

Hints, Cautions, and Tricks

☑ DO use the Force Field diagram in dealing with issues where you know or have a sense that making a change is the right thing to do

☑ DO be deliberate when stating the general issue above the two columns.

☑ DO carefully gather the early, rich conversation that results from discussing what could be done to overcome the Restraining Forces.

☑ DO the Force Field diagram on a flip chart so it is easy to transfer the information to computer or hard copy.

☑ DO recognize and capitalize on the concept that forces relate to movement, energy, and change. See the Force Field tool in that context.

☑ DO note how many times individual forces are mentioned within the group as the consolidated Force Field is developed on the flip chart.

☒ DON'T presume that the number of forces in either column is an indication of whether to proceed or not.

☒ DON'T be surprised at the conclusion that you will be able to affect most of the items in the Restraining column.

☒ DON'T judge or comment about the forces as they are being written down initially.

"Don't wait until everything is just right.
It will never be perfect. There will always be challenges,
obstacles, and less than perfect conditions. So what.
Get started now. With each step you take, you will grow
stronger and stronger, more and more skilled,
more and more self-confident, and more and more successful."
—Mark Victor Hansen

Gantt Chart

What is it?

A Gantt Chart is a graphical planning tool used to consider the tasks, their duration, and timing required to complete a project. It is also used to manage the project and to compare actual experience to the plan.

Why should I use it?

- Fosters commitment to a project and its completion if developed as a team
- Allows management to easily see the status of the project and to react before it gets behind schedule
- Enhances learning so planning for the next project will be better
- Makes it evident that some tasks in a project can be done simultaneously with others, and that some tasks cannot start until others are finished

When should I use it?

- To plan and manage a project
- To indicate who has responsibility for what tasks and therefore to assist in managing workloads
- To provide a visual representation of the plan and its progress for communication purposes
- To make an overwhelming project more feasible by breaking it down into manageable tasks.

Examples of use in a library setting

The library is researching or installing a new computer system.

The library is developing a Constancy of Purpose statement.

The staff is developing and carrying out a strategic plan.

The Director and supervisors are planning professional development.

Step-by-step instructions

1. Draw a horizontal line representing the expected duration of the project and divide it into time increments like days, weeks, or months.

2. On the left, along the vertical axis, list the tasks to be accomplished, the person responsible, planned start date, and estimated duration of the task. Note that the task may not take as long to do as the time over which it will or can be done.

3. Draw in bars representing the duration of each task. Draw them beginning at the starting date listed. If the bars are drawn as an outline, they can be filled in as the actual project is accomplished. Remember that weekends have to be considered when drawing the bar lines.

Success story

Charting the Collaborative Digital Project

When the folks at the Washington Research Library Consortium applied for a grant from the Institute for Museum and Library Services to develop a collaborative digital collections

SCHEDULE OF COMPLETION

	OCT	NOV	DEC	JAN	FEB	MAR	APR	MAY	JUN	JUL	AUG	SEP

YEAR 1 — 2001 ... 2002

- INITIATE PROJECT — $34,638
- CONFIGURE SYSTEMS — $25,714
- PLAN CONVERSIONS — $13,970
- CONVERT COLLECTIONS — $66,246
- DEVELOP GUIDEBOOK — $13,970

YEAR 1: $154,530

YEAR 2 — 2002 ... 2003

- SUPPORT SYSTEMS — $26,742
- PLAN CONVERSIONS — $5,085
- CONVERT COLLECTIONS — $117,106
- DEVELOP GUIDEBOOK — $24,922
- EVALUATE PROJECT — $9,581

YEAR 2: $183,436

TOTAL: $337,974

production center, they discovered that one of the requirements was to submit a Gantt Chart showing the schedule for completing the grant. It fell to Lizanne Payne, Executive Director for Strategic Planning and Budgeting, to develop the Gantt Chart. Payne had no special software, so she used Microsoft Word to develop the chart. In addition to showing the major categories of activity and the expected timetable of their implementation, the grant team wanted a way to show the relative cost breakdown of the project. They did this by putting the cost per category on the chart as well. Another embellishment on this chart was the use of dark bars that show active periods and lightly shaded bars that show periods of inter-mittent activity.

Payne said they are perfectly happy with using the chart for a high level description of the multiyear project. They have created subordinate schedules for day-to-day management of the project.

Hints, Cautions, and Tricks

☑ DO use a verb-noun format for naming tasks, e.g., "design workstation" or "research and order computers."

☑ DO keep the tasks to a manageable number—fifteen or twenty maximum. If more tasks are necessary, use subordinate charts.

☑ DO include a column on the chart for the individuals responsible for the tasks.

☑ DO mark on the chart when significant milestones need to be accomplished.

☑ DO use days on the time line for projects of three months or less. For longer projects use weeks or months. And for very short projects use hours.

☑ DO fill in actual progress and revise the chart frequently to reflect the actual status of the project.

☑ DO note that Gantt Charts are somewhat limited in project detail. They can be done by hand on graph paper or by using a computer. Generally it is best to keep them simple.

☑ DO make a list of the tasks, the person responsible, and expected duration of the task before putting all the information into Gantt Chart format.

Group Norms

What is it?

Group Norms are rules of operation that define how a group has decided to manage its work.

Why should I use it?

- Makes explicit what behaviors are expected and appropriate in a group
- Shifts responsibility for the operation of the group from the facilitator or convener to the group as a whole
- Allows any member of the group to remind another of failure to meet the expectations and behaviors expected of all members

When should I use it?

- To set ground rules for a committee, task force, work team, or learning group, usually at the first meeting
- To revisit the group's ground rules at the beginning of each meeting, and perhaps at the end

Examples of use in a library setting

The library serves as the convener for the community literacy council's organizational meeting.

A team chartered to develop a web site for the library holds its first meeting.

Staff from different library departments are meeting to revise the library's circulation procedures.

The presenter at a multiple-day training series involves the participants in setting the ground rules for the sessions.

Step-by-step instructions

1. Early in the first meeting of any working group, using a piece of chart paper or overhead or some other procedure that allows everyone to see, ask the group to help you establish the norms for your work together.

2. As participants suggest norms to be included, write them, using the participants' language as much as possible.

3. When the group has exhausted its ideas, wait a few seconds to be sure, then consider whether the group has covered all the essential points. If not, suggest other norms that you feel must be addressed.

4. Check for group agreement, then remind participants that they should try to follow the norms and that, if someone is not following them, any participant should bring it to the attention of the group.

5. From time to time, during the working meetings of the group, return to the norms and ask the group to assess how well it is doing. Ask if participants still agree the norms are appropriate. Add, delete, or revise norms as necessary.

Hints, Cautions, and Tricks

☑ DO involve the members of the group in developing the norms. To save time, the convener sometimes starts the discussion by contributing one or two ground rules, but the group must always concur and have a chance to offer additional points.

☑ DO share the norms with new members joining the group and ask if they agree or have any additional norms to suggest.

☑ DO encourage members to reflect on how their actions compared with the norms, perhaps at the end of the meeting.

☒ DON'T forget to include the ground rules in the minutes of the meeting and to post them or refer to them at each succeeding meeting so that participants know what they are.

Success story

Ground Rules for Learning

On the first day of a three-day continuing education series on marketing, presenter Sara Laughlin shared the results of her e-mail survey of participants before the first session and reviewed the objectives for the series. She explained that there would be three sessions and that after the first and second sessions, participants would have work to do in their libraries in order to practice and begin using the skills they were learning.

She asked the forty participants to help set ground rules for their learning. She started by suggesting one and writing it on the flip chart paper at the front of the room:

Start and end on time.

She asked the group to suggest others. They added:

Everyone participate.
Listen carefully.
Do our homework.
Be comfortable.

After suggestions had ceased, Sara waited a moment. Then she said, "These will be our rules. If you think of others at any time, don't hesitate to bring them to our attention. If anyone thinks we're not following our rules, please let us know that."

At the beginning of each session, Sara reminded the group of the norms. During the wrap-up at the end of the first day, one participant commented: "I noticed that lunch took a long time. Could we all try to get back on time next month, so we don't lose valuable learning time?" The group agreed to hold lunch to 30 minutes. Before the third session, one participant called and confessed: "I know we committed to doing our homework, but we've had two staff members resign, and we won't be able to complete it this time. What should we do?" Sara advised her to come and participate, so she could hear what other participants had accomplished. She reflected that these actions both showed that participants had taken ownership of their learning and their partici-pation. Rather than complaining about a too-long lunch break or dropping out because their homework wasn't done, they addressed the issues and sought help in making improvement.

Histogram

What is it?

A Histogram is a bar graph that shows the frequency and distribution of data.

Why should I use it?

- Displays the variation within a process—whether there is large or small variability or whether the data are skewed one way or another

When should I use it?

- To identify problems and opportunities for improvements
- To measure if a process conforms to a certain standard or stays within specifications
- To gather data for a Consensogram (p. 37)

Examples of use in a library setting

The library director wants to look at the age distribution or years of service of all employees.

The circulation staff wants to analyze the distribution of overdue fines collected.

The research department wants to analyze its responsiveness from time of inquiry until an answer is provided.

The processing team wants to investigate the distribution of repair costs per item.

The AV department studies the number of times a videotape circulates before it is worn out.

The children's programming team creates a visual picture of attendance at programs.

Step-by-step instructions

1. Collect the data. You don't need to put the numbers in any order. For our example, 3, 6, 4, 9, 5, 1, 6, 2, 5, 3, 7, 1, 8, 3.

2. Count the number of data points collected. In our list, there are 14 data points.

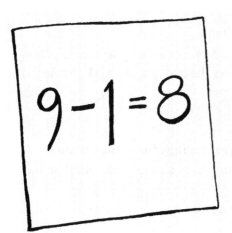

$$= 14$$

3. Compute the range of the data (A). Subtract the smallest value from the largest value. In our list, for example, the smallest value is 1 and the largest 9, so the range is 8.

$$9 - 1 = 8$$

4. Determine the number of classes (B), using the chart below, which has been developed through experience. Use it as a "rule of thumb." For example, if you have 14 data points, as in the example above, you would want to divide your graph into five classes.

No. of Data Points	No. of Classes
25 or fewer	5
26-50	7-10
51-100	11-13
101-250	14-20

5. Determine the class width (C). The Range (A) divided by the number of classes (B) yields the class width (A/B=C). In our example, 8/5=1.6. For simplicity's sake, it is usually easiest to round to the next whole number; in our example, 1.6 would be rounded up to a class width of 2.

6. To determine the class boundary, round the smallest value to the next lower suitable number, then add this number and the class width together. In our example, the lowest number is 1, so we will use that as the lower boundary. The first class will include all numbers between 1 and 2.9 and we will create boundaries at 3 (up

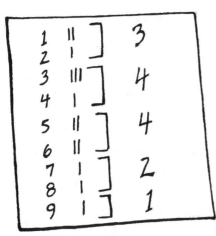

to 4.9), 5 (up to 6.9), 7 (up to 8.9), and 9 (up to 10.9), which gives us the five classes, with boundaries evenly spaced.

7.   Construct a frequency table by tabulating how many numbers fall within each class. For our example, the table at left is an illustration. The numbers on the left are all the numbers in the data set. The "hash marks" following each number represent the number of times each number appears. The brackets combine them and create a total within each of the class boundaries set in Step 6.

Class No.	Class Boundary	Frequency	Total
1	1 – 2	xxx	3
2	3 – 4	xxxx	4
3	5 – 6	xxxx	4
4	7 – 8	xx	2
5	9 – 10	x	1

8.   Construct the Histogram based on the frequency table. On the X axis, represent the classes. On the Y axis, show the frequencies.

9.   Study the Histogram to gain an understanding of the results. Typical Histograms follow a bell-shape similar to the one in the illustration to the left. The number of days items are checked out, for example, would form a bell-shaped curve, with the highest frequencies near the due date and diminishing numbers of items returned very early and very late.

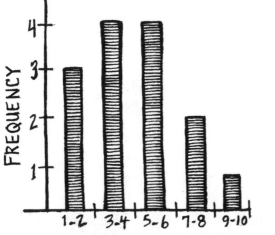
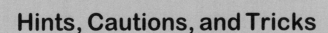

Hints, Cautions, and Tricks

☑ DO try to collect 20 points of data before constructing the Histogram. More data will yield a more reliable picture.

☒ DON'T expect Histograms to always follow a bell-shaped curve.

Success story

Wells County's Recreational Library Use Follows the Curve

As part of their strategic planning, the Wells County Public Library conducted a survey, in which they asked their patrons why they used the library. Two hundred and sixty-one of the respondents checked categories, including "Recreation and Leisure." The survey also gathered demographic data including age, in five- and ten-year increments aligned with the U.S. Census.

Director Stephanie Davis, with the assistance of consultant Jane Raifsnider, decided to plot the data in histogram form. They had 261 data points, ranging from the youngest age group (5 to 9) to the oldest (75 and up). When they looked at the census divisions they had used on the survey, they realized that some spanned five years and others covered ten years. They were forced to combine into ten-year divisions, in order to have parallel class widths. That meant that they had eight classes, a few less than the fourteen suggested as a minimum in Step 4 of the instructions.

They constructed a frequency table:

Class	Class Boundaries	Frequency
1	5-14	11
2	15-24	20
3	25-34	46
4	35-44	68
5	45-54	56
6	55-64	26
7	65-74	17
8	75+	17

Based on the frequencies, they created a Histogram. They noticed that the library's users of recreational and leisure materials followed a "bell curve."

"We were a little surprised by the picture," mused Davis. "We had assumed that our older patrons were the heaviest consumers of leisure reading. We're not done investigating yet, but the Histogram certainly caused us to ask lots of questions." For their next steps, they plan to create a similar Histogram of the population of Wells County, using the 2000 census, by ten-year increments, hoping to see whether the pattern of library use follows the population pattern or whether certain age groups are under- or over-represented. They will also compare the overall survey

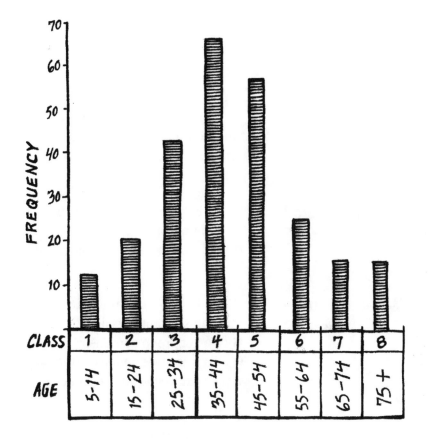

responses with the census breakdowns, to see if the survey itself was representative of the county population as a whole.

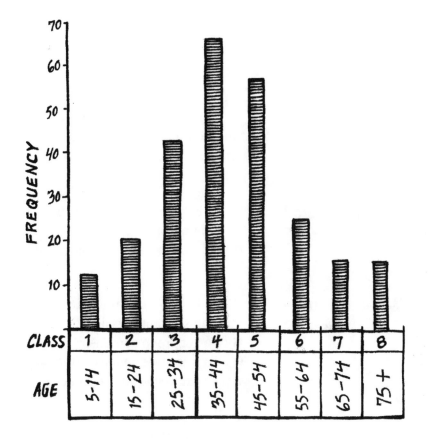

"Data, plural of datum,
derives from the Latin word daius,
which means what is given,
hence gift, present."
—Webster's New World Dictionary

Multivoting

What is it?

Multivoting is a way to efficiently reach consensus about the most popular or important item(s) on a list.

Why should I use it?

- Helps a group gain consensus when needs are diversified and opinions are varied
- Allows equal power and input from each member of the group

When should I use it?

- To help a group prioritize a large number of ideas after a brainstorming session
- To get group consensus
- To prioritize options without creating a "win-lose" situation
- To reduce the numerous items in a long list to a manageable few

Examples of use in a library setting

A department prioritizes work assignments, based on the library's strategic plan.

A team gives priority to possible causes of variation in a process.

The program committee chooses its favorite new programs from a brainstormed list.

The children's department determines which new or ongoing services to offer.

Step-by-step instructions

1. Decide on the aim of the session.

2. Generate a list of items, using Brainstorming (p. 15) or another tool. Combine similar items; you could create an Affinity Diagram to do this (p. 7). Number the items on the list.

3. Give each person stickers or sticky dots equal to one-third the total number of items being considered to use as votes. If there are fewer than ten issues, give each person three dots or stickers. Give each person one "hot dot," usually red, for his or her most important issue. (In the story below, see a modification which allowed participants to indicate their most important issues and to flag those which were most problematic.)

4. Ask individuals to vote for their preferred choices by putting their dots or tick marks, if stickers are not available, by the items of their choice. Note: It is acceptable for an individual to invest more than one vote on an issue.

5. Tally the votes for each item. The highest priority may or may not be the issue with the most hot dots. Use the results to inform the group's discussion.

6. Repeat the process to narrow long lists to a manageable few.

Hints, Cautions, and Tricks

☑ DO use a group facilitator who can remain neutral throughout the process.

☑ DO use stickers or sticky notes to make voting fast and visible. Tally marks or numbers can also be used.

☑ DO use the Nominal Group Technique (p. 77) instead, when participants are unable to meet in person or when the issue is very contentious.

Success story

Refining Actions, Building Support

The staff of the Dubois County Contractual Public Library was meeting for a daylong action planning session to create an action plan for the library's strategic plan. A planning committee made up of community members, board, and a few staff representatives had been hard at work for several months, conducting focus groups, gathering data, and creating a mission, vision, and values for the library. They provided the staff with these documents, as well as draft goals and objectives. In the morning, the facilitator led the staff through Brainstorming (using sticky notes, see Brainstorming Option 3, p. 17). For each objective, they identified dozens of actions the library could take, some of them quite creative. By noon, a dozen pieces of chart paper with action ideas were taped around the room.

The facilitator used Multivoting to help the staff sort the ideas into four categories. She gave each person five stickers of each of the four colors and directed them to walk around the room and study the ideas before "voting" as follows:

- Green (go) for those powerful ideas that should be implemented immediately because they would help advance the library's mission, vision, or values.
- Blue for good ideas that should also be implemented during the next three years.
- Yellow (caution) for areas where the library should proceed with caution.
- Red (stop) for ideas that the library should not implement.

Within a few minutes, the staff had prioritized the ideas, and they—as well as the facilitator—could see which ideas had strong support and which were troubling to the staff.

After lunch, the staff broke into small groups to refine the actions for each objective. The colorful stickers allowed each small group to work with confidence that the action plans they were creating were reasonable and would have support from the other groups who were working in different rooms on different parts of the plan. The facilitator helped each group remember to focus on the mission, vision, and values of the library, rather than their own comfort and convenience, as they finalized the plans. By the end of the afternoon, the library staff cheered as each group reported on its section of the action plan.

Nominal Group Technique

What is it?

Nominal Group Technique is a structured process that helps a group select and rank problems, choices, or issues that need to be addressed.

Why should I use it?

- Provides focus or identifies high priorities when a group is diversified or an issue is highly controversial
- Provides each team member with an equal voice

When should I use it?

- To prioritize and generate a course of action when group members are working from different sites or when a large group of people need to be involved
- To reduce errors in group decisions

Examples of use in a library setting

Faced with limited program funding and staff, the library team prioritizes programs offered by each department.

The library narrows a long list of possible values by polling the staff and ranking results.

Step-by-step instructions

Part One: Formalized Brainstorming

1. Define the task in the form of a question.

2. Describe the purpose of the discussion.

3. Clarify the question and provide additional explanation if group members need clarification.

4. Generate ideas, using any of the techniques of Brainstorming (p. 15).

5. Clarify the ideas listed, combining any that are duplicates, perhaps using an Affinity Diagram (p. 7).

Part Two: Selection of Ideas

6. If more than fifty items are listed, identify a process to reduce the number. Use Multivoting (p. 74) to limit the list or allow team members to remove less important items on the brainstorming lists. Note: It should be the "originator" of the idea who volunteers to remove it from the list at this point.

7. Number or letter the remaining items on the list.

8. Give each participant four to eight votes. Do this by giving each participant pieces of paper or 3" x 5" cards (votes) based on the following guidelines:

> four votes for twenty or fewer items
> six votes for twenty to thirty-five items
> eight votes for thirty-five to fifty items

9. Ask each group member individually to make his or her selections and vote. Provide one card per vote when using Nominal Group Technique in a meeting or use e-mail ballots if a group is not in the same location at the time of the vote. Ask each member to put the number or letter corresponding to the item under consideration on a voting card. On the same card place the ranking of its importance. The least important item will receive a 1. For example, in a four-vote system, the most preferred item would receive a 4, the second most important item would receive a 3, etc., and the least preferred item would receive a 1.

10. Tally the votes. The item that receives the highest point total is the group's selection.

11. Review results and discuss the reaction. If time allows, display the results in a Pareto Chart (p. 91) to illustrate which items received the most votes and which items received the most points. Note: Sometimes the two are not the same. It is possible for an item that is strongly preferred by a few people to receive the most points, while another weakly preferred by many people receives the most votes. Use this information to generate discussion.

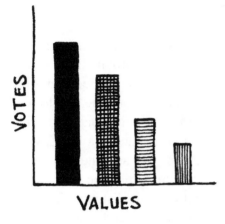

Hints, Cautions, and Tricks

☑ DO carefully plan and prepare as the facilitator.

☑ DO allow for discussion if the top priorities are distributed.

☑ DO limit using Nominal Group Technique to a single-purpose meeting. It is difficult to change topics in the middle of the meeting.

☑ DO understand that this technique is called "nominal" because it doesn't require as much interpersonal interaction—in fact, it is often implemented using e-mail or mail voting—as most group techniques.

☑ DO note that this tool offers a more formal, structured system for developing consensus than others like Multivoting (p. 74). In some instances, more than one round of Nominal Group voting takes place, as the group progressively narrows its focus. For example, a national group creating recommendations might use the Nominal Group Technique via e-mail to narrow its list, then send the resulting list as a survey to a much broader group of respondents and ask them to prioritize again.

Success story

Identifying Top Ten Trends, via E-mail

Sara Laughlin was responsible for planning a program for a national conference. She decided to use the opportunity to increase communication with members who could not come to the conference and to build interest in the conference program. She sent a query to a discussion list of consortia directors around the country and asked them to nominate a trend for inclusion in the program on "top ten trends affecting library consortia." It could be, she told them, a trend that affected their network or one they had noticed in their communities or their own lives. In the space of a few days, she received more than forty nominations. She sent them to her informal advisory committee and they helped combine similar ideas and eliminate duplicates. She returned the list, now including twenty-six trends, to the listserv subscribers and asked them to choose and rank their top six. Within days, she received more than one hundred responses. People were so enthusiastic about the project and curious about the final list that Laughlin began to get inquiries: "What are the top ten?" "Can I get them in time for my board meeting next week?" "Will the list be published anywhere?"

Laughlin tallied the votes. Each respondent had marked a "6" for the most important trend, a "5" for the next most important, and so on. Every trend was ranked by at least one person; a few received top or near-top rankings from almost every respondent. The top ten trends were:

> Complex, rapidly changing electronic environment
> Restructuring work
> Complete rethinking of education
> Growth in buying clubs and cooperatives
> High demand for skilled workers
> Diversifying funding
> Collaboration, partnering, and community building
> One-stop shopping
> Accountability for results
> Demand for extraordinary services

Following the well-attended conference program, the Association of Specialized and Cooperative Library Agencies Publications Committee Chair asked if Laughlin could make the presentations into a book. The ten trends became ten chapters written by consortia directors.

Operational Definition

What is it?   An Operational Definition describes what something is and how it is to be measured.

Why should I use it?
- Reduces variation in measurements when a team agrees on what they are measuring and exactly how they will measure it
- Reduces failed expectations between suppliers and customers

When should I use it?
- To provide foundation for continuous improvement
- To save time and money
- To come to agreement with suppliers and customers
- To provide clear definitions for job expectations
- To eliminate waste

Examples of use in a library setting

The library includes operational definitions in its contract for support from an automation vendor.

The personnel handbook defines "on time."

The library board and staff develop a policy defining who is eligible for a library card. The policy takes into account state law, as well as local practice.

The library adjusts its record-keeping to align with newly developed operational definitions for the state library annual report.

Step-by-step instructions

1. Establish the need for an operational definition and, for first time users, define in general terms what an Operational Definition is.

2. Begin with one person proposing his or her Operational Definition for the situation.

3. Others concur, question, or propose an alternative Operational Definition.

4. Continue until all parties agree, then put the Operational Definition in writing for future reference.

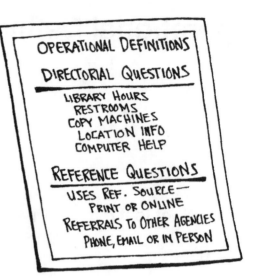

OPERATIONAL DEFINITIONS

DIRECTORIAL QUESTIONS

LIBRARY HOURS
RESTROOMS
COPY MACHINES
LOCATION INFO
COMPUTER HELP

REFERENCE QUESTIONS

USES REF. SOURCE —
PRINT OR ONLINE
REFERRALS TO OTHER AGENCIES
PHONE, EMAIL OR IN PERSON

Hints, Cautions, and Tricks

☑ DO get group input to have true meaning and agreement. All parties need to be involved.

☑ DO be creative in thinking about the many possibilities for misunderstanding when creating an Operational Definition.

Success story

State Library Simplifies Reporting by Sharing Definitions

In January, when the Indiana State Library collects statistics from Indiana public libraries for the annual report, consultant Edie Huffman knows that she'll get daily questions about operational definitions. She has done several things to help those in the 239 public libraries around the state who are completing the report over the Internet. She includes the operational definitions in the online help, even though "many people don't read the definition before asking a question." Last year, she began sharing answers to frequently asked questions about Operational Definitions in a statewide discussion list.

Most of the data required on the annual report is set by the Federal-State Cooperative System (FSCS) for Public Library Data, which supplies operational definitions. The State Library cannot change the FSCS definitions, but it can—and often does—elaborate on them.

A good example is the data element "number of library programs." Library staff submitting the statistics have asked Edie, "Does the program have to be sponsored by the library?" and "What about programs held in our meeting rooms which are planned and presented by outside groups?"

For children's programs, the FSCS definition says, "Count of audience at all programs for which the primary audience is children. Includes adults who attend programs intended primarily for children."

The American Library Association added an operational definition of "children:" "individuals 14 years of age and under."

The Indiana State Library further elaborates: "It is not necessary that the program take place at the library to be counted. A program that is planned, sponsored, or carried out by library staff is a library program. If there are a series of programs, such as story hours, where the same people attend each program, record the attendance at each program. For example, if the same ten children attend three separate story times, you should report a total attendance of thirty. Count everyone who attends any program, no matter what age group. Please begin collecting data on programs according to these age divisions, if your library does not already do so. Do not count dial-a-story or other phone-in programs. Include all outlets (central library, branches and bookmobiles)."

"You just have to keep working with the definition to figure out some other way to explain it or understand it," she notes. "On the national level, we keep having conversations about how to measure electronic usage. Even circulation is not as good a number as I would have hoped. How do different libraries handle books they check out to teachers? In some libraries, they treat that circulation just like that of any book. In others, teachers may count every time they let a child take it home or count thirty if they read the book to the entire class, and the library uses that count. It's always been hard to explain why there are libraries whose count is far above others of the same size with similar staff and similar collections. Now people at least are talking about it."

Pair and Share

What is it?   Pair and Share is a technique for engaging individuals in a dialogue in order to deepen understanding and arrive at shared meaning.

Why should I use it?
- Encourages reticent individuals to participate
- Shortens the process of gathering ideas from a large group
- Minimizes differences in knowledge, experience, or confidence
- Increases the number of ideas that can be generated and eliminates redundant ideas from a group

When should I use it?
- To digest and discuss new information
- To generate ideas during brainstorming
- To create shared definitions and reach consensus

Examples of use in a library setting

Library staff who work with young adults share new research that shows the impact of summer reading on student achievement with the whole staff.

The library's strategic planning committee, which includes community members, students, board, and staff members from all levels in the library, identifies trends that will affect the library in the next few years.

A State Library task force, convened to assist in developing new measures for library services, creates definitions to be included on the online data collection site.

Step-by-step instructions

1. Explain the activity to the group and ask each person individually to prepare for the conversation by, for example, reading the materials and making notes, or thinking of solutions to a problem, or writing a definition.

2. Find a partner (or two, if the group is very large), and share what you have read, learned, or written. Sometimes the facilitator will time the conversation and inform the group when it is time for the second partner to share. During the conversation, the two individuals question each other and clarify points that are not clear. Usually, the two partners combine their learning into a single final product. If they are writing a definition, for example, they might be asked to merge their two individual drafts into one final product. If they are brainstorming ideas, they might be asked to combine their lists and then add one more idea from their discussion.

3. At the end of the initial Pair and Share round, the pairs may either report to the group or join another pair and complete a second round of discussion, clarification, and merger of ideas.

Hints, Cautions, and Tricks

☑ DO provide specific instructions for the pairs.

☑ DO limit the time for the pairs to work and give them periodic reminders about how much time remains.

☑ DO use triads if the group is very large or there is an odd number of participants.

Success story

Bedford Builds Shared Values

The Bedford Public Library remodeling included merging children's circulation, formerly on the second floor, and the adult circulation, formerly on the first floor, into a single lower-level location near the new main entrance. The circulation manager needed to design the new area, rethink the circulation process, and forge a new team from the dozen or so staff members. She decided to begin by developing shared values, based on the three values recently created through a process involving the entire library staff:

> Honest
> Courteous
> Open-minded

At a staff meeting, each circulation staff member used a large strip of paper to write a draft definition for the first value. They used the Pair and Share process to share their draft definitions, discuss them, and arrive at a joint definition. Next they shared their joint definition with another pair and created a new shared definition. Finally, the three foursomes shared their definitions and the group combined and discussed them. The facilitator observed that some of each pair's work appeared in the "working" value sentences for the department:

> Honest: We feel trusted as individuals and we are always honest with our co-workers and the public.
> Courteous: We treat co-workers and the public with kindness and respect.
> Open-minded: We are accepting of people and receptive to new ideas and changes.

Dialogue during the activity was thoughtful, and the staff was well pleased with the results. One pair noticed that the values applied to staff interactions and another added that the values would also apply to board policies and library decisions as well as to customer service. Through their conversations, they deepened their own understanding of the values and added to the library's collective understanding.

Paired Comparison

What is it?

Paired Comparison is a group decision-making strategy used to help a group choose among several alternatives. This tool is sometimes called "forced choice" since it requires participants to choose between every good choice and every other good choice.

Why should I use it?

- Forces group members to make choices (Even when two alternatives seem equal, members must choose one. Having to make difficult choices often leads people to see advantages or disadvantages they may not have noticed before.)
- Shows the pattern of a group's preferences
- Stimulates discussion among group members
- Prioritizes a range of options or root causes

When should I use it?

- To help a group reach consensus
- To prioritize among a number of choices
- To allow interesting factors to surface for further discussion
- To identify the "critical few" root causes or key success factors

Examples of use in a library setting

The library's strategic planning committee identifies key success factors.

The technology team compares vendor responses.

The summer reading committee selects a theme.

The staff searches for the root causes of low morale in the library.

Step-by-step instructions

1. Agree on a short list of options. These could be root causes, key success factors, or possible solutions. In the left-hand column, list the choices under consideration. The technique works best with between six and twelve options. The options may have come from a variety of stakeholder techniques; see for example Brainstorming (p. 15). Sometimes it is necessary to use Multivoting (p. 74) or Nominal Group Technique (p. 77) to reduce the choices to a workable number.

2. List the options in no particular order and number them on a flip chart.

3. Ensure that the team is clear on the subject to be considered. If the team is analyzing root causes, the decision could be: "Which is the greater cause of the problem?" If the team is prioritizing solutions, the decision will be: "Which solution will fix or prevent the problem more effectively?"

4. Give each member a Paired Comparison Chart and ask him or her to fill in the subject name, and then to copy the options from the flip chart in the left-hand column, using exactly the same numbering.

5. Each individual completes the voting matrix on the Paired Comparison chart. Always start on the first row/first column and work across the row. In the box in the first row/first column, there are the numbers 1 and 2. This instructs the user to compare item 1 with item 2 and to circle the number that represents the greater cause of the problem or the better solution, depending on the application. In each comparison, each member has one and only one vote. He or she must decide which of the two alternatives is better. Everyone must cast a vote in each comparison, even if neither choice is very appealing. (The total number of votes cast in any comparison must equal the number of people in the group.)

6. Still on row 1, move to column 2 and repeat, this time comparing item 1 with item 3. Continue until row 1 is complete.

7. Move to row 2. Because the comparison between item 1 and item 2 was done in row 1, it is not repeated here, so this row is one comparison shorter and each succeeding row will also have one fewer set of numbers.

8. Continue until all rows are complete.

9. The user now adds up the score. For example, when adding up the score for option 1, all circled 1s are in the top row—a total of 2. One 2 is circled. No 3s are circled. For 4s though, the user must search in several rows, looking horizontally, before finding three 4s and entering that total

10. Complete the totals column on the right-hand side of the Paired Comparison chart.

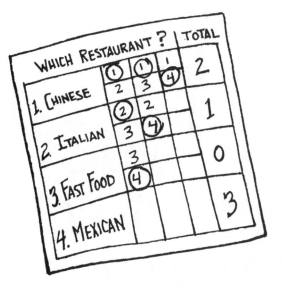

11. Collect all the individual scores onto the Totals Table and calculate total scores and rankings.

12. Present the results to the team for discussion, focusing on the areas of least consensus. Paired Comparison generates four pieces of information: the individual's score, the team's score, the team ranking, and the degree of consensus. Team totals should be used cautiously. If several options have similar scores, they should be considered together.

13. Histograms (p. 69) for each option show the degree of consensus in the team and are important for understanding some of the deeper issues. If the degree of consensus is high and the participants truly reflect the views of the stakeholders, this result can be considered reliable. The only danger is one of "group think," where the participants are so close to the problem that they have already convinced themselves of the issues. The facilitator should be aware of this possibility.

14. If little consensus is achieved, or the Histogram shows polarity, further investigation is required. Sometimes the disagreement arises because of confusion over definitions; other times it represents true differences of opinion. In these cases, focus on the areas of lack of consensus and get those who are at the extremes to explain their reasoning. Further evidence may need to be collected before consensus can be achieved. The team may wish to repeat Paired Comparisons to see if there is more agreement as a result of the discussion.

Success story

Participants Choose a Good Restaurant

Workshop participants practiced the Paired Comparison tool on a daily decision that is often frustrating for library staff—choosing a restaurant for lunch. They made a list of the nearby options they liked: Chinese, Italian, Fast Food, and Mexican. They wrote the choices on the left-hand side of their charts. Individually, they worked their way across the first row, asking "Between Chinese and Italian, which would I choose?" and circling their preferences. After they had each made all the choices, they totaled the selections in the right-hand column. When they added the group's totals, they discovered that Mexican was the clear choice.

Hints, Cautions, and Tricks

☑ DO remember that the comparisons are subjective, so the validity of the strategy will only be useful if the group proceeds in good faith.

☑ DO involve stakeholders throughout the whole improvement process, including Brainstorming (p. 15) and Multivoting (p. 74).

☑ DO use the data resulting from Paired Comparison to provide a focus for discussion rather than a final decision. The highest total on the Paired Comparisons chart does not automatically become the group's decision. The data does provide input to the process of deciding. In working toward consensus, the group can focus discussion on the two or three top options.

☑ DO produce a Histogram (p. 69) of the scores for each option, if you want to gain more information.

☒ DON'T pre-set the list of options to be prioritized.

☒ DON'T force a decision using Paired Comparison if the group is not ready to compromise.

☒ DON'T use Paired Comparison as a substitute for data collection and analysis. As a subjective, opinion-based technique, it is best used where precise cause-and-effect linkages are difficult to measure.

Pareto Chart

What is it?

A Pareto Chart is a visual representation of data arranged in order from most frequently occurring to least frequently occurring.

Why should I use it?

- Helps teams visualize which few causes account for most of the problems, so they can spend their time improving critical areas
- Provides an objective, comparative measurement of data collected on a problem or area that needs improvement

When should I use it?

- To help identify the most frequent causes of errors or problems, in order to decide where to focus improvement efforts
- To highlight the most important causes of success, to assure continued attention to them
- To study results of improvement efforts over time

Examples of use in a library setting

The circulation staff studies the reasons for returning materials late, drawn from a customer survey.

The strategic planning committee studies the estimated costs of rectifying library complaints.

The technology team studies a staff survey to identify the highest priorities for improving the library automation system.

The technical services department tries to pinpoint the most common ordering errors.

Step-by-step instructions

1. Choose the problem or issue to be studied. Using Brainstorming (p. 15) or existing data that have been collected, determine general categories into which the data can be divided.

2. Decide on a common unit of measurement such as frequency or cost.

3. Determine a time period over which the data have or will be gathered.

4. Gather the data and put into a Check Sheet (p. 33) format.

5. Draw a graph with the unit of measure on the vertical (Y) axis and the list of categories from left to right in order of descending frequency on the horizontal (X) axis. ("Other" is always presented last, even if its total is larger than that of other categories.)

6. Above each category, draw a bar representing the measure of its frequency or cost.

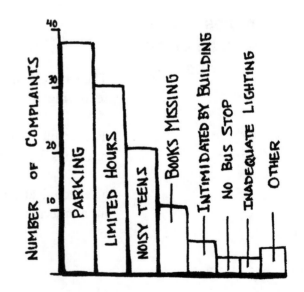

Success story

Libraries Study Customer Complaints

Before one of the CI learning sessions, the participating libraries gathered customer complaints. At the session, they studied all the complaints and created seven main categories, which they listed on a Check Sheet (p. 33). They added "Other" and decided to put any complaints that didn't fit neatly into categories there. Next, they made a hash mark in the appropriate category for each complaint.

When they had finished the Check Sheet, they created a bar graph, starting from the largest category on the left to the smallest, with the last on the right reserved for "Other."

Even though the exercise involved several libraries, it was obvious that the complaints from their customers were remarkably similar and that, if they could resolve issues of parking, hours, and noisy teens, they could eliminate a huge percentage of the complaints.

They combined the Cause-and-Effect Diagram (p. 25) and the Cause Analysis (p. 21) tools to search for root causes.

Hints, Cautions, and Tricks

☑ DO remember that the identification of problem areas will only be as good as the categories into which the data are clustered.

☑ DO use common sense in choosing where to begin work. Sometimes the most frequently occurring cause is very difficult or out of your control to do anything about. Conversely sometimes less frequently occurring causes are extremely important or are so easy to fix they are obvious choices.

☑ DO be certain to separate dissimilar causes. For example, when studying reasons for arriving at work late, the response "overslept and couldn't find parking" should be separated into two categories, "overslept" and "couldn't find parking." While oversleeping might not be something that the library could improve, inadequate staff parking might be able to be resolved.

☑ DO remember to carefully label the Pareto Chart with a title, date completed, time period over which the data represented were collected, and the name of the person who did the chart.

Parking Lot

What is it?

The Parking Lot is a tool that is used to gather and retain ideas that may be valuable in the future.

Why should I use it?

- Captures all potentially valuable ideas
- Improves efficiency of the group
- Validates everyone's ideas and participation
- Offers an anonymous way for people to communicate

When should I use it?

- To retain ideas, comments, or questions which arise that are not specifically on the subject being worked on at this meeting or planning session
- To capture thoughts so they will not be overlooked or forgotten or when discussion of these ancillary thoughts would be distracting or too time-consuming
- When participants have questions or comments that might be embarrassing or controversial

Examples of use in a library setting

A team is developing a flowchart of an existing process and someone comes up with an idea of how to make the process better.

A training session is under way and someone asks a question that is slightly off subject or would require a great deal of time to answer. The presenter can get together with the questioner during a break or at a later time to discuss or answer the question.

During a problem-solving session someone comes up with an "off the wall" great idea that pertains to an entirely different issue.

Step-by-step instructions

1. Prior to the gathering or during if it is not done beforehand, write "PARKING LOT" at the top of a flip chart page.

2. Explain the purpose of the Parking Lot to the group and encourage them to use it.

3. The facilitator or anyone else in the group can simply say, "I think that is an idea for the Parking Lot."

4. The facilitator or a volunteer writes the idea on the Parking Lot sheet or on a sticky note for posting.

5. At the end of the meeting or during a break, review the Parking Lot ideas and decide who has the responsibility to do something with each of the ideas listed.

Hints, Cautions, and Tricks

☑ DO make sure something is done with all of the items listed on the parking lot—if only to evaluate and discard them.

☑ DO write down the exact words or make sure the person giving the comment is satisfied that what is written down captures the essence of the idea.

☑ DO make sure that what is written will be understandable a few days later.

☑ DO consider the Parking Lot a legitimate way to deal with a participant who keeps bringing up a pet issue or with a participant who is determined to be disruptive.

Success story

Parked But Not Forgotten in Brownsburg

When the Brownsburg Public Library's continuous improvement team met for their first meeting, they established Group Norms (see p. 66). Most of the team had attended the Fishbowl meeting (see the Fishbowl success story on p. 47) and clearly realized that many process improvements could or should be made to improve accuracy in shelving.

The team quickly reached consensus on the need to narrow their process master to a specific collection in the library. They chose to work on adult fiction first. They revisited the variations in standards between the adult and junior collections, as well as rediscovered the many processes that occur prior to shelving an adult fiction book. Many suggestions for overall improvement in shelving were expressed. Needing a secure place to park those good ideas for future examination and implementation, they used the Parking Lot. Some of the issues that ended up on the Parking Lot list follow:

- Should both junior and adult fiction be in series (numerical) order as opposed to author/title order?
- If there is variation in the junior department shelving standard, then junior staff should inventory the junior collection.
- Pay attention to what you're doing when shelving.
- Change fiction call numbers to five letters.
- Mini-pages (grade school volunteers) may need to be retrained.
- Secure shelf labels in the junior department.
- Consider department-specific pages.
- May need to add more maneuverable book carts.
- Remind all staff to return empty book carts to the sorting room.
- More training and follow-up training with our pages.
- Establish ownership and pride in the workplace.
- Must do sorting process to define timeliness.
- Buy and install more shelves.

The Parking Lot worked. The CI team was able to move forward with the narrow focus of shelving adult fiction books, while assuring team members that their good ideas would not be lost.

Plus/Delta

What is it?

A Plus/Delta chart is a tool that is used to get feedback from people about what went well and what could be improved in a given situation.

Why should I use it?

- Yields quick feedback, while the meeting is still on participants' minds
- Determines what was good or positive about a meeting, training session, or other situation
- Elicits what could be changed or improved the next time
- Gives all participants an opportunity to express their opinions
- Situates ownership of the meeting with the whole group, not just with the facilitator or team leader

When should I use it?

- To get an understanding of how something is going or how it has gone, normally at the conclusion of a meeting, but it can be used during a meeting to make mid-course corrections

Examples of use in a library setting

A board evaluates its meeting.

Staff reflect on a multiday program after the initial session.

Participants consider strengths and areas of improvement for a training session.

A team considers how effective they were in solving a problem.

Step-by-step instructions

1. Draw a large "T" on a white board or flip chart page. Label the left side with a large "+" and the right side with a large "D."

2. Ask participants, "What went well today?" Write down their comments verbatim on the "+" side.

3. Ask participants, "What could we have done better, or what should we change for the next time?" Write these comments on the "D" side.

4. Return to the top of the "D" side and discuss the suggestions. Can we make a simple change for next time? Does this require a major change? Do we, as a group, really want to make this change? Will this cost a lot of money? Will this take a long time? Who will take responsibility?

5. Prior to the next meeting or event, reflect on the results of the previous Plus/Delta and adjust accordingly.

Success story

Carmel Captures Ideas for Improving Young Adult Summer Reading Programs

The seven members of the young adult department of the Carmel Clay Public Library met in mid-August to celebrate the success of their various summer activities and to capture everyone's ideas about what had worked and what had not worked in their two summer reading programs. (For a description of the two, see page 102.) They knew they would not have a lot of time at this meeting, but they wanted to meet as a whole group one last time before their two summer assistants went back to college.

Plus/Delta was a perfect tool for capturing a lot of information quickly. One person wrote everything down on a large

98

paper that everyone could see. Each person said everything he or she could think of that had worked well ("+") and everything he or she could think of that might need to be changed ("D").

Plus

- For the first time this year, we counted all kinds of reading—not just chapter books but also magazines, graphic novels, and picture books (as when teen babysitters read aloud to their charges).
- There were approximately 1,000 participants (i.e., good participation, a slight increase from last year).
- Bookstore gift certificates were wildly popular as prizes.
- Teen Library Council members chose the hilarious theme: "I Pity the Fool Who Don't Read!"
- Teen Library Council provided artwork for the reading logs.
- Teens provided input on prizes during the planning stages.
- People liked getting the $1-off-library-fines coupon for signing up.
- All staff felt more comfortable going into the summer having had a training session of their own in the spring.

Delta

- Get more (and more structured) input from Teen Library Council members regarding prizes.
- Include more bookstore gift certificates as raffle prizes.
- Have a *weekly* raffle prize for the regular summer reading program as well as for the college-prep summer reading program
- Develop more—and more mutually beneficial—partnerships with local businesses. This year, we were pressed for time and were fortunate enough to be able to just buy most gift certificates to use as prizes, but next year we may not have as much money to spend.
- Ask the library's coffee shop owner to donate coupons.
- Not requiring college-prep teens to write book reviews did not seem to increase participation. (Last year they had to write reviews, but the total participation was about the same both years.)
- Offer a book list that college-prep teens can take home.
- Ask high school teachers to offer extra credit to students

who participate in the college-prep program.

■ Consider lowering the 3000-page limit for both programs, if we care about increasing our completion rate.

■ Consider offering only one program, since so few teens do the college-prep program.

■ Entering names in all caps was annoying; instead, when training the Teen Volunteer Corps summer assistants, stress the importance of spelling names correctly in the database.

■ Stress that volunteers notice when participants are nearing the 3000-page limit.

■ Change the database program to flash a message and block entry after 3000 pages.

■ Write the number of Book Bucks earned next to each title in participant's reading log, in ink.

Hints, Cautions, and Tricks

☑ DO celebrate and reinforce the positive items listed.

☑ DO write down the exact words.

☑ DO take the opportunity, as a facilitator, to discuss and clarify the real meaning of the comments made.

☑ DO discuss, as appropriate, how an improvement will be made, and who will do it. This is a valuable step that is many times overlooked.

☑ DO type up the Plus/Delta and distribute it to participants. By so doing there is memory of what happened and what assignments were made.

☑ DO use the Plus/Delta even with a very large group. Ask individuals to list their "Plus" comments on sticky notes. These can be gathered and compiled into a Check Sheet. Do the same for the "Delta" side to collect ideas about things that could be changed or improved.

☒ DON'T forget to do the Plus/Delta. Even though it is generally at the end of a meeting, and the meeting may be running late and people are tired, it is important to allot time to this important tool.

- What to do with kids who try to cheat?
- Do we need to be more flexible about the five-book-per-day limit?
- Do we need $10 Book Bucks (in addition to $1 and $5)?
- End on a Saturday or Sunday instead of on a Friday; lots of parents were surprised this year.
- Post a countdown clock—"X number of days left in the summer reading program."
- Promote the programs earlier, with eye-catching signs.
- Offer more attractive prizes for finishing.
- Have written evaluation forms available for participants and parents. We heard lots of appreciations. One parent asked if she could fill out an evaluation because she loved our programs so much; we didn't have a form ready to capture and record all the enthusiasm.

Hope Baugh, head of the young adult department and facilitator for the Plus/Delta exercise, offers these tips for using the Plus/Delta tool:

- "Do it as soon as possible after the event ends about which you are capturing information. Because of staff vacations, we could not meet as a department until three weeks after the summer reading programs had ended, and people had already mentally moved on to other things. Next year, I will not wait for a formal department meeting, which is often difficult to arrange. Instead, during the last week of the summer reading programs, I will put up a large paper in our YA workroom, make two columns on it, and record Plus/Delta notes as I chat informally with each staff member. I will also encourage people to jot down what occurs to them on their own.
- "Make sure the notes are detailed enough to understand weeks later. We have 'Ilya's trick' as a plus, but I no longer remember what that means!"

The staff did not have time at this meeting to evaluate or incorporate the suggestions. The five year-round members of the YA department planned to meet again later in the fall to begin working on next year's programs, using the information they gathered at this meeting.

They also did not spend a lot of Plus/Delta time on the Teen

Volunteer Corps' activities, although they were another big part of the library's summer, involving every young adult staff member and closely related to the summer reading programs. Instead, coordinator Karen Burrow and summer assistant Rachael Levin presented a detailed summary evaluation at the meeting, and the department chartered an interdepartmental team to "process master" how summer Teen Volunteer Corps tasks are solicited, scheduled, supervised, and evaluated. (See Charter p. 28.) The process mastering will take several meetings.

"I would like to use the Plus/Delta tool at those meetings, too," noted Baugh.

She offered this description of the two summer reading programs offered by the young adult department: "The regular one ('I Pity the Fool Who Don't Read!') was for people going into grades 6-12, and the college prep one ('Alt-readers'), for people going into grades 9-12. People had to choose one or the other.

"In the regular program, participants could read anything they wanted. They earned a 'Book Buck' for every 50 pages read, up to 3000 pages. They could spend their Book Bucks on small prizes or on raffle tickets towards larger prizes that would be awarded at the end of the summer. They could also write book reviews to earn raffle tickets. People who reached 3000 pages received bookmarks to encourage them to keep reading. They also received raffle tickets towards the grand prize raffle: a $50 gift certificate to a local bookstore.

"In the college-prep program, participants had to choose their books from *Reading Lists for College-Bound Students: Getting a Head Start on College Success* by Doug Estell, Michele L. Satchwell, and Patricia S. Wright, 3rd edition (Arco Publications, 2000). Four reference copies of this book were available at the YA desk. For every 50 pages read, participants earned a raffle ticket. Each week, someone won a $20 gift certificate from a different local store. Anyone who read 3000 pages got to pick a trade paperback as a prize and received a raffle ticket towards the grand prize raffle: a $75 gift certificate to a local bookstore."

"Without learning,
there is no survival.
Survival is not compulsory."
—W. Edwards Deming

Process Behavior Chart

What is it?

A Process Behavior Chart is a graphic tool used to study variation in a process over time.

Why should I use it?

- Helps leaders determine whether and when to take action
- Assists library board members, administrators, and staff in learning about and measuring variation in a library process
- Identifies and distinguishes common and special causes of variation in a process
- Allows organizations to make predictions about what will occur in the future
- Provides a visual picture that helps employees improve processes by eliminating special causes of variation, reducing common causes of variation, and improving the average outcome, to better meet customer needs

When should I use it?

- To see if a process is in-control (predictable) or out-of-control (unpredictable)
- To monitor the stability of a process over time
- To improve processes and outcomes

Examples of use in a library setting

The branch librarian wishes to understand and predict daily attendance in order to schedule staff and routine maintenance.

The maintenance staff wants to lower utility usage in order to reduce costs.

The circulation department wants to reduce shelving errors.

Step-by-step instructions

There are several types of process behavior (control) charts designed for different purposes. The authors have chosen to discuss one type, which will apply to most situations found in libraries. It is known as the X and Moving Range (MR) Chart for Individuals. For those who want to know more about control charts, please consult the references listed in the Further Reading section.

To construct an X and MR Process Behavior Chart, use a chart similar to the one on page 106 and complete the following steps for the data you have collected. The example used in the instructions below comes from the Benton County Public Library, whose story follows the instructions and whose data were used to create the charts on pages 106 and 109.

1. Begin by filling out the known information at the top of the chart for your process.

2. Write down the date (and time, if appropriate) and the data points (X's) for the most recent 20-25 measurements. If you have fewer points, use what you have. The Benton County Public Library used two years' worth of monthly data.

3. Choose an appropriate scale and plot and connect the points on the X/Sample graph. Remember to leave space for the upper and lower natural process limits. At Benton County Public Library, the largest monthly number of packages handled was 117 and the smallest 17, so they chose to use increments of 20 on a scale from 0 to 180. (For more information, see Run Chart, p. 111.)

In the next five steps, move to the lower chart to plot and connect the Moving Range points and calculate the Moving Range average and its Upper Process Limit, a number which will then be used in computing the Upper and Lower Process Limits in the upper chart.

4. Calculate the moving ranges (MRs). Find the difference in value between the first and second X and pencil it into the Moving Range (MR) row. Benton County did this by subtracting the February 2001 total of 16 packages handled from the January 2001 total of 26. They entered "10" in the first MR box. Do the same for points 2 and 3, 3 and 4, etc. Note that it is the absolute difference between the numbers that is important. Therefore don't worry if you get a negative number. Write it down as a positive number.

Choose an appropriate scale, as in Step 3, and plot the points on the Range chart at the bottom of the page.

5. Calculate the average $\overline{MR}$. Add up all the MR values and divide the total by the number of MR's to get $\overline{MR}$. Place the $\overline{MR}$ value in the blank at the top of the page, and draw a dashed horizontal line at that value on the Moving Range chart. At Benton County, the total was 533, which they divided by 23, for an $\overline{MR}$ of 23.17.

6. Calculate the Upper Process Limit for the Moving Ranges (UPL_{MR}) by substituting into the following formula:

   $UPL_{MR} = \overline{MR} \times 3.267$ Write this value in the blank at the top of the page.

Benton County took its $\overline{MR}$ of 23.17 and multiplied it by 3.27 for an UPL_{MR} of 75.70.

7. Check for special causes in X's. Are any MR's greater than the UPL_{MR}? If the answer is yes, delete the X that is out of whack and calculate a new $\overline{MR}$ and a new UPL_{MR}. If no, continue to calculate the standard deviation (S).

8. Calculate the standard deviation (S) as follows:

   $S = \overline{MR}$ divided by 1.128 Write the value of S in the blank at top of page.

Benton County divided 23.17 by 1.128, for an S of 20.54.

Using the standard deviation from Step 8, return to the upper control chart to find the average of X values and compute the Upper and Lower Process Limits.

9. Calculate the average of the X's ($\overline{X}$). Find the sum of all the X's and divide that total by the number of X's. Write this value in the blank at the top of the page, and draw a horizontal line on the X/SAMPLE chart at the value of $\overline{X}$. At Benton County, the total of the 2001 and 2002 monthly figures was 1486, which they divided by 24 to get 61.92.

X and Moving Range Chart

PROCESS NAME __PACKAGES HANDLED__

UNIT OF MEASURE __COUNT__

PROCESS OWNER _____

DATE CALCULATED __9/10/02__ BY WHOM __SGL__

$\overline{X}$ __61.92__ UPL$_X$ __123.54__ LPL$_X$ __.3__

$\overline{MR}$ __23.17__ UPL$_{MR}$ __75.70__ S __20.54__

DATE		JA	FE	MA	AP	MY	JE	JL	AU	SE	OC	NO	DE	JA	FE	MA	AP	MY	JE	JU	AU	SE	OC	NO	DE	TOTALS
DATA	X	26	16	42	34	17	51	51	66	117	52	34	86	54	51	105	98	59	72	77	68	89	90	56	75	1486
	MR	10	26	8	17	34	0	15	51	65	18	52	32	3	54	7	39	13	5	9	21	1	34	19		533

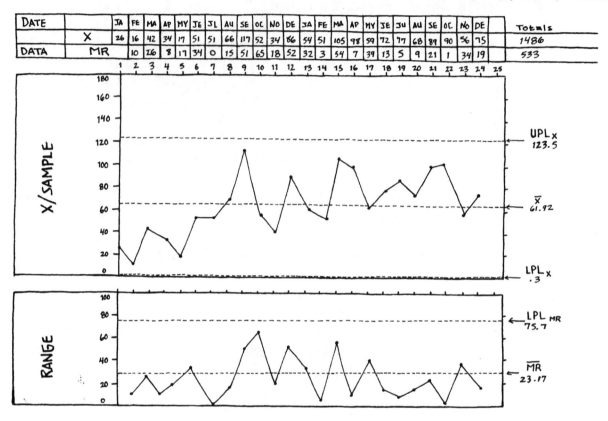

10. Calculate the Upper Process Limit for the X's (UPL$_X$):

$$UPL_X = \overline{X} + 3S$$

Draw a dashed horizontal line on the X/SAMPLE chart at the value of the UPL$_X$. Benton County added 61.92 and 3 x 20.54 (61.62) for a total of 123.54.

11. Calculate the Lower Process Limit for the X's (LPL$_X$):

$$LPL_X = \overline{X} - 3S$$

Draw a dashed horizontal line on the X/SAMPLE chart at the value of the LPL$_X$. If LPL$_X$ is a negative number, draw the LPL$_X$ at 0 on the graph. The UPL and LPL serve as the "boundary lines" separating "common cause" variation from "special cause" variation.

Benton County found its LPL_x by subtracting 3 x 20.54 (61.62) from 61.92, for a total of .3.

A process team expects to see points falling between the control limits. Up-and-down fluctuation within the limits is normal and expected. By studying the chart, team members can determine if there is little or large variation. They can assess whether the average is higher or lower than their customers expect.

When points fall outside the control limits, they are called "special cause" variation. Usually these points can be explained by unusual circumstances. Perhaps the library was closed due to an ice storm or the computer was down. Maybe a press release about a library program caused unusually heavy traffic on the web site for a few days.

12. Analyze what your process is telling you. Is the process "predictable" or "unpredictable?" Is there a great deal of variation? Is the average higher or lower than your customers expect? Is your process getting better, getting worse, or staying about the same? Does your process go through cycles?

Success story

Benton County PL Takes a Closer Look at Package Shipping Process

Marie Brown at the Benton County Public Library had the sense that she was packaging more books for interlibrary loans as time went by. She even had monthly data showing the numbers going back to January 2001. She knew how many packages she shipped and how many packages she received.

It wasn't until she actually plotted the data on the first Process Behavior Chart, however, that she visually confirmed what she sensed—that the number of packages shipped per month was going up over time. (See illustration on p. 106.)

Benton County Public Library is a small library, and the number of packages is not all that large. Nevertheless Brown estimates that she spends 4 percent of her time (1° hours/week) dealing with this chore. And this is only the packaging time, which doesn't include gathering and dispersing the books.

Another thing that the data showed was that the number of packages shipped (and interlibrary loans) jumped in the July/ August 2001 time period, when the library consortium to which Benton County belongs put their catalog on the Internet and dramatically improved the ability of library patrons to see holdings of the consortium's libraries and borrow them. When Brown saw that the first seven points were below the average line, while almost all those since August 2001 were above the line, she knew that her system had indeed shifted. She recalculated the average and Upper and Lower Process Limits for the January-July 2001 and August 2001-December 2002 periods separately and plotted them on a second Process Behavior Chart to more easily study the new system now in place. (See illustration on p. 109.)

When she looked at the Moving Range Chart at the bottom, she saw that the Moving Range before the system change was narrower than that after the change. Right after the change there were a few months of wild variation, but in a few months the variation had narrowed as the new system settled into place and staff and patrons became comfortable with its capabilities.

Brown showed the Process Behavior Chart to some of the other libraries in the consortium and asked them to plot their data. The Thorntown Public Library staff members who handle interlibrary loans confirmed that they had also seen a substantial increase and promised to share their data with Brown. She expects that their system—and probably that of all the consortium libraries—will show the same jump after mid-2001. If they do, she'll have further evidence that the new web-based catalog has been well-received by patrons all over the consortia. "None of the libraries has publicized this new service, but it looks like some of our patrons have discovered it anyway," she said.

Brown's next endeavor is to track the time she spends to do the whole chore from beginning to end on a weekly basis. She is convinced that unless she finds ways to be more efficient, this job will soon require additional part-time help. When and if that is necessary, she feels she will have the data in a format that will be convincing to her board.

"To change the way that you create a product, change when, how, and with whom you share information."
—Fara Warner

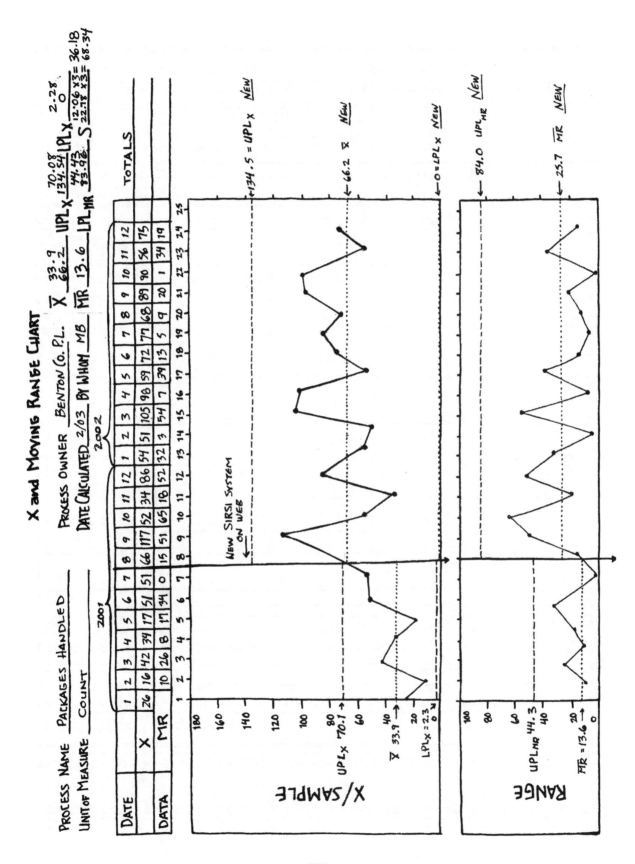

X and Moving Range Chart

Process Name Packages Handled
Unit of Measure Count

Process Owner Benton Co. PL.
Date Calculated 2/03 **By Whom** MB

$\overline{X}$ 33.9 UPL$_X$ 70.08
$\overline{X}$ 66.2 UPL$_X$ 134.54 LPL$_X$ 2.28 / O
$\overline{MR}$ 13.6 LPL$_{MR}$ 44.43 / 93.92 12.06 x3= 36.18 / 22.18 x3= 68.34 S

DATE		1	2	3	4	5	6	7	8	9	10	11	12	1	2	3	4	5	6	7	8	9	10	11	12	TOTALS
				2001													2002									
DATA	X	26	16	42	34	17	51	51	66	117	52	34	86	51	105	98	59	72	77	68	89	90	56	75		
	MR	10	26	8	17	34	0	15	51	65	18	52	32	3	54	7	39	13	5	9	20	1	34	19		

X/SAMPLE

New SIRSI System → on web

← 134.5 = UPL$_X$ New
← 66.2 $\overline{X}$ New
← O = LPL$_X$ New

180
160
140
120
100
80   UPL$_X$ 70.1 →
60
40   $\overline{X}$ 33.9 →
20   LPL$_X$ = 2.3
0

RANGE

← 84.0 UPL$_{MR}$ New
← 25.7 $\overline{MR}$ New

100
80
60
44.3 UPL$_{MR}$
40
20   $\overline{MR}$ = 13.6 →
0

109

Hints, Cautions, and Tricks

DO understand that the process limits help process managers discriminate between common and special causes. They can predict with 99.7 percent assurance that, unless the process is changed, future data points will fall within the calculated natural process limits established by plus or minus three standard deviations above and below the mean of data gathered about the process.

DO remember that special causes are not always indications of problems. They may have occurred because of weather or other factors beyond the library's control.

DO plot at least 20-25 data points, in order to have confidence in your predictions.

DO remember it is most effective to have the process owner or workers plot the points on the process behavior chart.

DO note that a process is considered to be "predictable" if data points vary randomly above and below the mean (average) over time and if no points fall outside the upper or lower natural process limits.

DO note that a process is considered to be "unpredictable" if data points fall above or below the natural process limits, if 7 or more consecutive points lie on one side of the mean, or if a series of 7 or more consecutive points continues to rise or fall.

DO calculate new natural process (control) limits after you have made an intervention to improve your process, and your data confirm that your process has changed.

DON'T have a computer generate and track data on a Process Behavior Chart, even though it is tempting. It is much more valuable to have the individuals put the dots on the chart. (Great librarians plot points.)

DON'T treat common cause variation as if it were special.

DON'T treat special cause variation as if it were common.

Run Chart

What is it?	A Run Chart visually represents data over time or in sequence.
Why should I use it?	■ Shows variation in a process ■ Shows the average of the data
When should I use it?	■ To see trends and shifts in the data ■ To present data as input for a Process Behavior Chart (p. 103) ■ To monitor progress after making changes in a process
Examples of use in a library setting	The circulation staff charts circulation by location, by hour, and by collection category, over time. Reference librarians in each branch plot reference questions answered by category, over time. The library creates a report of phone calls received at each desk. The library charts improperly discharged items on a monthly basis. The human resources plots staff sick days per week or month.
Step-by-step instructions	1. Write the title of the Run Chart and other pertinent information at the top of the page. 2. Create and label X and Y axes with the measurement on the Y axis and the time or sequence on the X axis. Choose a scale for the Y axis that represents existing and expected future data and that fits the page you are working on.

3. Using data points gathered, plot the points on a graph in a single line, from left to right, even if the data represent more than one year.

4. Connect the data points with a line.

5. Calculate the average (mean) of the data by adding up the values of all the data points and dividing the sum by the number of data points.

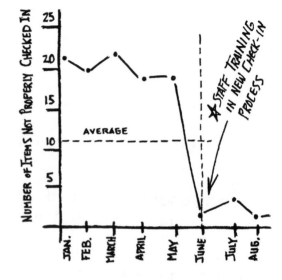

6. Draw a horizontal line representing the average on the Run Chart.

7. Study the Run Chart for clues about the process it represents.

Success story

Mooresville Reduces Book Check-in Errors

The Mooresville Public Library had a problem with improperly discharged books, which caused a significant amount of dissatisfaction for customers and rework for the staff. Several times a month, customers would receive overdue notices for books that they had already returned. Needless to say, they were not happy and their impression of the library was deteriorating. Staff members had to take the irate calls, only to walk to the shelf and find the book there, with the date due card still inside.

The library decided to find out how often this problem was really occurring. They created a Check Sheet (p. 33) at the circulation desk so every staff member could note when this problem occurred. At the end of each month, they totaled the numbers. They plotted the monthly totals on a Run Chart. After four months, they knew that their present system was yielding an average of more than twenty-one improperly discharged books each month.

Since the library is small, almost everyone is involved in

circulation, so they created a process master at a staff meeting. Next, they Brainstormed (p. 15) improvements. By the end of the meeting, they had dramatically simplified the process and added a second confirming discharge, since their automated system was sometimes unreliable. In addition, they made some simple physical changes in the circulation area. They moved the circulation center away from the return book cart at the circulation desk, so patrons would be less likely to add their newly returned books to the carts of already discharged books waiting to be shelved.

They painted one book cart red, signifying "Stop! These books have not been discharged!" and placed it in a convenient location for customers. They painted another one yellow and placed it by the discharge station, so staff would know that these books had been discharged once but ("Caution! Not ready yet!") were waiting for the second discharge.

The improvements took an afternoon. The next month, only four books were improperly discharged. The library has tracked the data for eight months since the process improvements were completed. The Run Chart shows that the number of improperly discharged books has declined to an average of four per month, an 81 percent reduction.

After six months, the Mooresville staff reviewed the process master, looking for ways to reduce the mistakes even further. Reflecting on their first attempt at creating a Run Chart, the library realized that, if they were going to do a better job next time, they would factor in the number of books handled per month and compute the error rate. If, for example, they handled 1000 books in the month and misshelved 21 (the average before improvement), the error rate would be .021 or 2.1 percent; after the improvements the error rate dropped to 0.4 percent. The numbers would be different each month depending on total books handled and errors.

Hints, Cautions, and Tricks

☑ DO be on the lookout for important cycles, trends, or runs in the data, e.g., 7 points in a row above or below the average or 7 or more data points in a row that continually increase or decrease. These are important indicators that something significant has changed.

☑ DO carefully label the Run Chart with a title, date, and who initiated it. If warranted, describe how the data are measured. See Operational Definition (p. 81).

☑ DO understand that Run Charts are most useful to the person who is working with the process or responsible for the process. Therefore it is most powerful for that person to plot the points on an ongoing basis.

☑ DO consider that the faster you gather data, the greater your opportunity to learn about and improve your process.

☑ DO understand that even though computers can create Run Charts efficiently and print them neatly, the power of the Run Chart is most often experienced with a pencil and a piece of paper.

☒ DON'T be fooled into thinking that every variation in the data is important.

"You only get better results if you have a better method."
—Brian Joyner

Scatter Diagram

What is it?

A Scatter Diagram is a plot of two variables used to graphically display a possible relationship.

Why should I use it?

- Determines if there is a correlation between two variables
- Displays what happens to one variable when another variable changes

When should I use it?

- To validate "hunches" about a relationship between two variables
- To determine the direction of a relationship between two variables
- To interpret the strength of a relationship between two variables
- To test for possible cause-and-effect relationships
- To show trends
- To choose among alternatives

Examples of use in a library setting

Program planners determine the relationship between program attendance and library use.

The library technology team displays the relationship between web use and circulation.

The children's department works with a local elementary school to determine the relationship between summer library use and grades.

The library's continuous improvement team plots library processes and key success factors in order to determine which processes will yield the most impact if they are improved.

Step-by-step instructions

1. Collect and construct a data sheet of paired samples of data.

2. Create a summary table of the data.

3. Draw a diagram labeling the horizontal and vertical axes. Generally the values on the axes should get higher as you go up and to the right.

4. Plot the data pairs on the diagram by placing a dot at the intersections of the X and Y coordinates for each data pair.

5. Add quadrants to the chart by drawing a vertical bar down the graph at the halfway point and a horizontal bar across in the other direction.

Process	Key Success Factors			Importance (Add across A+B+C)	Condition (Good = 5; Poor = 1)
	A Lifelong Learning	B Recreational Reading	C Community Space		
Catalog materials	5	5	1	11	3
Answer reference questions	5	5	1	11	1
Offer photocopy service	3	1	5	9	5
Do payroll and accounting	3	3	3	9	4
Write board reports	3	5	1	9	4
Send overdue notices	3	3	1	7	2
Circulate materials	5	5	5	15	3
Shelve materials	5	5	5	15	2
TOTAL	32	32	22		

Success story

Dunkirk Decides Where to Work

The Dunkirk Public Library had identified three key success factors to guide it over the next few years:

Contributing to lifelong learning and information
Supporting recreational reading
Providing comfortable community spaces

To help them reach these goals, the library pinpointed eight important processes. They listed them in the left-hand column of the chart. Next, they used a scale of 1 to 5 to evaluate the importance of each process to achieving each key success factor. They asked, for example, "How important is cataloging materials to lifelong learning?" and decided that it was very important, so they gave it a "5." They worked across each row until they had finished filling in the chart. Then they added across each row to find the total and entered it in the "Importance" column.

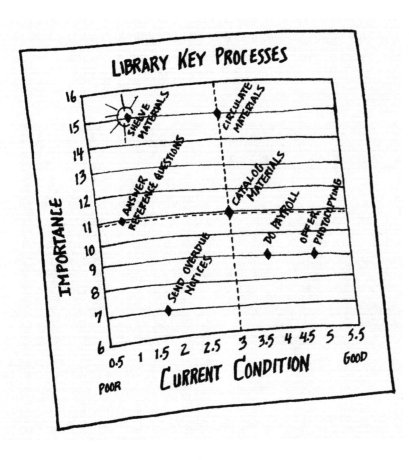

Finally, they assessed the current condition of each process, using the same scale of 1 to 5, with 5 being "good condition" and 1 being "poor condition" and entered the condition rating for each process in the far-right column.

By studying the table, they could see which processes were most important and which ones were in worst condition. By adding the numbers down the key success factor columns, they also noticed that one of the key success factors had a lower score than the other two, an indication that they might need to review their processes to see if they were strong enough to achieve this key success factor or whether they might need to create additional processes in this area.

They created a Scatter Diagram by plotting the importance totals against the current condition numbers. When they divided the Scatter Diagram into four quadrants, it was easy to see which processes they should work on. "Shelve materials" appeared in the upper left quadrant because it was very important to achieving the library's key success factors and was in relatively poor condition. "Circulate materials" and "Answer reference questions" were the next most important processes. With a staff of two assistants and limited resources, Director Ailesia Franklin was happy to be able to focus on the processes that would be most likely to lead to immediate improvement.

Note: This story illustrates an unusual use of a Scatter Diagram where each set of variables is unrelated to each other set. Normally there are just two variables and the Scatter Diagram shows the strength of the relationship between the two variables.

Hints, Cautions, and Tricks

☑ DO interpret data patterns, whether in a positive or negative direction, for strength by examining the "tightness" of the clustered points. The more the points are clustered to look like a straight line, the stronger the relationship.

☒ DON'T assume that the existence of a relationship means cause-and-effect. A third variable may be responsible.

"Our goals can be reached
through a vehicle of a plan,
in which we must fervently believe
and upon which we must vigorously act.
There is no other route to success."
—Stephen A. Brennen

Visual Synectics

What is it?

Visual Synectics involves using pictures to trigger ideas and emotions, often as part of brainstorming, reflection, or change efforts.

Why should I use it?

- Provides concrete visual images for scaffolding thinking
- Is non-threatening
- Stimulates metaphoric thinking and gets to the heart of the content quickly
- Appeals to those who learn and operate in the physical and emotional worlds

When should I use it?

- With a newly formed group, to help them focus on the topic at hand
- In the early stages of brainstorming, to help trigger more inventive ideas
- As a wrap-up, to help individuals recall key concepts or ideas
- To create a vision or feeling

Examples of use in a library setting

The strategic planning committee, made up of library board, staff, and community members, meets for a visioning session. The session opens with a visual synectics exercise, as the facilitator passes out photographs on cards and asks: "How are these pictures like the library of the twenty-first century?"

A group of newly hired staff wraps up a day of orientation by selecting an object from a basket and comparing it with one of the library's policies.

Step-by-step instructions

1. Prepare one or a set of picture cards—photographs of everyday objects cut from magazines or catalogs. A mix of organic and human-made objects seems to work best. You may choose to project a single image for the whole group to see. As a variation, try using small objects instead of pictures. Give each person an object and ask him or her to describe how it is like the topic at hand, or ask participants as a group to examine and pick an object from a basket and discuss and decide how it is like the topic.

2. If you are using multiple cards, structure groups of three or four. Randomly distribute cards to each group or let them draw one from a pile placed face down.

3. Have the small groups generate responses to an open-ended question posed by the facilitator, e.g., how is (your topic or issue) like (your picture card)?

4. Small groups then compare their lists to the topic or concept selected by you for comparison.

"The real act of discovery consists not in finding new lands, but in seeing with new eyes."
—Marcel Proust

Success story   *Painting a Mind Picture*

During the first morning of the Continuous Improvement
Initiative, participants were introduced to several new concepts,
including system thinking and continuous improvement. When
they opened the afternoon session, the presenters projected a
photograph of a beautiful mountain vista. In the picture, trees were
tinged with red and yellow in the foreground and faded into
luminous violets on the peaks and warm shadows in the valleys as
they receded into the distance. The scene, familiar and yet non-
specific, conjured up pleasant associations. The presenters asked the
participants to study the picture. "How does it look like continuous
improvement?" they asked. After a few minutes, they answered:

"The mountain scene is like continuous improvement
because it is an unending journey."

"Each leaf is part of a tree and each tree is part of a hillside,
but when viewed together, they create this beautiful
landscape. In the library, the interactions of every task and
process every day impact the quality of our system."

In just a few minutes, the facilitators knew that participants had
understood the main ideas from the morning.

Hints, Cautions, and Tricks

☑ DO laminate the cards to make them more durable.

☑ DO use easily understood pictures that depict or imply something going on (avoid
abstract patterns, etc.).

☑ DO aim for a wide variety of content, feeling, and simplicity/complexity, but
preferably with neutral or positive associations rather than negative ones (despair,
anger, revulsion).

☑ DO use pictures that display scenes unconnected with the actual task at hand.

☑ DO choose pictures that are open to various interpretations, so that participants can
imagine their own scenarios for what is happening.

Why-Why

What is it?

Why-Why is a simple but powerful technique that is used to get to the root cause of a problem.

Why should I use it?

- Takes some of the emotion out of problem-solving
- Increases efficiency in analyzing a problem
- Improves the odds that you will actually solve the problem

When should I use it?

- To get to the bottom of what is really causing the problem
- To analyze the problem at the time the problem presents itself

Examples of use in a library setting

The staff wonders, "Why are we always running out of paper towels in the bathroom?"

Her supervisor wants to understand why Mary is always late for work.

The community wants to know why is it so difficult getting good board members.

The staff wonders why books aren't on the shelves when they are supposed to be.

Step-by-step instructions

1. Clearly state the problem or situation.

2. Ask why this is happening or why this condition exists.

3. State the answer.

4. Then ask another "why" question based on the previous answer.

5. Continue this pattern until you have reached the root cause of the problem.

Success story

The Root Cause of Paper Jams

Participants in the Continuous Improvement Initiative tried their Why-Why skills on an everyday problem in most libraries.

"Why do we have paper jams?" asked facilitator Ray Wilson.

"Because we use poor quality paper," they answered.

"Why do we use poor quality paper?" continued Wilson.

"Because it's cheaper," came the reply.

"Why do we use cheap paper?" he continued in his third question.

"Because we waste a lot of paper," they continued.

In his fourth question, Wilson wondered "Why do we waste so much paper?"

"Our patrons don't know to set print jobs correctly," they said.

"Why don't patrons set their print jobs correctly?" he returned in his fifth "why" question.

"They haven't been trained," they replied.

With just five rounds of "why" questions, they had arrived at the root cause of paper jams.

123

Hints, Cautions, and Tricks

☑ DO think carefully how to phrase the "why" questions.

☑ DO ask the why questions out loud, with inflection in your voice.

☑ DO avoid suggesting that the problem is caused by a person. At least 90 percent of all problems are system problems, not people problems. Remember this is Why-Why, not Who-Who.

☑ DO understand that this tool is sometimes called "the five whys" because usually by the time you have asked the question five times you will have found the root cause of the problem. Sometimes you will have solved the problem with fewer than five whys. Sometimes it will require asking "why?" more than five times.

☒ DON'T be dismayed if this tool doesn't lead to a cause the first time. Usually this happens because of improper phrasing of the why question. When this occurs, begin again and ask different, carefully considered why questions.

"The formulation of a problem is the most essential part of problem solving."
—*Albert Einstein*

Using the Tools in a Continuously Improving Library

Most of the tools included in this volume are not new. Nor are they complicated or time-consuming. Nevertheless, their use can dramatically change the way library staff members—or any task group, for that matter—work together. The change is the result of profound shifts. First, the tools help staff members begin to tackle long-standing problems. Second, the tools help people focus on library processes rather than personalities. Finally, they provide simple mechanisms through which libraries can include their customers and suppliers in efforts to improve.

In the stories below, three libraries describe how they applied continuous improvement tools to the issues they were confronting.

Plainfield Public Library used the tools to address issues of daily operation, including "claims returned" items, declining registration for the summer reading program, cataloging local history materials, and assessing the impact of new Sunday hours. They included their patrons and were thrilled by their suggestions and unexpected positive comments. All of these efforts were under way at the same time.

Jeffersonville Township Public Library applied the tools to various aspects of planning for a renovated and expanded facility. They began by involving their staff in clarifying the library's mission, vision, and

values, and identifying key success factors and key processes to support them. They are using other tools for creating calendars for the complicated planning tasks and for assessing their readiness for the move to a temporary location.

Bloomfield-Eastern Greene County used continuous improvement tools to help the library consortium in which it participates make decisions about where to work and how to assign tasks. By incorporating these simple tools, they simplified the consortium staff's difficult decisions about where to spend their time, gave guidance to the automation system supplier about which issues to address first, and reduced competition among consortium members for attention to their needs.

Plainfield Uses Tools to Involve Staff and Patrons in Gathering Ideas for Improvement

At the Plainfield Public Library, staff are using continuous improvement tools to improve programs, daily processes, and cooperation between departments.

As the circulation staff considered a mission for their department, they realized that they were the first point of contact for library patrons. "Service begins with us," they decided. Next they turned their attention to identifying root causes of one of their biggest problems—too many "claims returned" items were being found on the shelves, after patrons had received overdue notices. They used a **Cause-and-Effect Diagram** to identify all the possible causes, one of which was improper or incomplete check-in. They decided to study the check-in process, but meanwhile they added a second check-in procedure, in hopes of reducing the problem. "We've seen a decline already," noted Reann Poray, circulation department head.

In the children's room, the staff agreed that their mission was "Connecting kids at the library." They decided to use continuous improvement tools to tackle an emerging problem: declining participation in their summer reading program. In about half an hour at a staff meeting, they used the **Force Field Diagram** to list the forces that were motivating patrons to participate and those that were restraining their participation. Once they had a long list, they used **Multivoting** to determine which restraints were most important.

They involved their patrons in their efforts as well. Placing the list of possible restraints, a form of **Check Sheet**, on an easel next to the children's circulation desk, they asked patrons whose children had not participated to place sticky notes (*Multivoting*) on the reasons listed on the easel. The conversations that took place were rich, according to department head Theresa Lucas, and one of the unexpected results was that patrons whose children had participated asked the staff to add a second sheet where they could add their comments in support of the summer reading program.

After about a week, the staff created a **Pareto Chart** of the restraints, which clearly showed them where they needed to make improvements next year. Most of the restraints were things that the library could control, and the staff had many ideas for improvement. Ideas also came from parents. For example, one of the largest restraints was the limited registration period. Several parents complained that they had tried to register early, since they knew they would be on vacation during the official sign-up; the staff had not been able to accommodate them.

In their planning for next year's summer reading program, the staff will incorporate many of the suggestions from staff and patrons. They have already committed to contacting teachers to ask them to be more involved in promoting the program with parents and children. They will also work more closely with day-care centers and home school families.

Library director Char Skirvin tried out continuous improvement tools on cataloging Indiana materials, a process that involved the cataloging department and the Indiana Room staff. Over the years, Indiana Room staff had complained that the cataloging department took too long to catalog their materials, most of which needed original cataloging. The process had not changed, even though the library's new automated system would allow the Indiana Room staff to participate in cataloging. Skirvin used a **Charter** when she asked a team, including staff from both departments, to create a process master. They

"Success is a journey, not a destination. The doing is usually more important than the outcome."
—Arthur Ashe

used a ***Top-down Flowchart*** to show the movement of materials and decisions involved. "I keep checking," she reports, "It worked. There's been no tweaking. I think involving the people who own the process was the key to developing a workable solution."

Meanwhile, she's plotting data on a ***Run Chart*** about the number of patrons, number of new cards, and circulation on Sundays, to confirm that the library's new Sunday hours are effective. "We already knew that Sunday hours accounted for 7 percent of our open hours. We learned that we were circulating 8 percent of our total items and issuing 7 percent of our total new cards on Sundays. The Run Chart helped us see the patterns and the upward trends in use. We're planning to use these figures as a benchmark; as we make changes, we'll be able to see if they are improvements."

Jeffersonville Uses CI Tools to Prepare for Construction Project

Learning about continuous improvement tools came just in time for Bill Bolte and the staff of the Jeffersonville Township Public Library. "It changes your overall thinking," Bolte noted. "Our group works differently now. We're using the tools at every level, from planning our new building to improving our daily processes."

First, the library defined its mission, vision, and values. The staff continuous improvement committee ***Brainstormed***, starting with the existing mission and goal statements. They used ***Nominal Group Technique*** in a survey distributed to the entire staff to get input on values. Staff were asked to rank five values statements based on the validity of each statement, key words, and

their relationship to the newly conceived mission and vision. Top-ranking values were:

Accessible. We ensure facilities whose staff and materials are accessible.
Knowledgeable. We employ knowledgeable staff to fulfill the needs of our patrons.
Respectful. We are respectful and courteous to all individuals.
Responsive. We are responsive to the expectations of our changing community.
Welcoming. We provide staff and an environment that are welcoming to all.

The new mission, vision, and values guided the library staff in its building program as they began to meet with the library architect and associates to plan an expansion and renovation that would truly make the library "a dynamic community destination."

The library identified four key success factors which would help them carry out their mission, reach their vision, and maintain their values:

Popular programming and diversified collections
Cutting edge technology and facilities
Competent and friendly staff
Positive long-term relationships with customers

Next, they charted the key success factors and library processes using the key processes matrix. When they plotted the resulting points on a ***Scatter Diagram***, they could clearly see the relationship of each key success factor to current library processes. The Scatter Diagram helped the committee decide which of the processes they should subsequently focus on improving. "Staff training" was at the top of the list of key processes needing improvement.

Meanwhile, in the adult services department, there was the perception of an ongoing problem with reserves. "We used the *Why-Why* tool and it worked very well. We thought staff might be resistant, but they drilled down very quickly to the root causes. Next, we used the *Force Field Analysis* tool to identify what was holding us back. We were falling down in getting items to the right branch," said branch manager Kathy Rosga. "Another problem was that staff in non-circulation departments could place a hold, but they were not enabled to change patron information, so sometimes the telephone number or address would be wrong, and we weren't getting the information."

For consistency, the library staff created a *Deployment Flowchart* for training staff so that every staff member who interacts with the public would be able to place holds and to update patron records. The change also eliminated a step for patrons; they would no longer have to go to more than one service desk to place a hold (reserve).

When working on the building project, they created a *Gantt Chart* to show the time line and responsibilities for each person in establishing a bond issue to finance the renovation and expansion project—a complicated process involving several people over a period of months with tight deadlines dictated by the library Board meeting schedule.

"Nothing is particularly hard if you divide it into small jobs."
—Henry Ford

As they prepare to move to a temporary facility for a few months, the director has **Chartered** teams to prepare for the various aspects of the move, to guarantee that library customers are informed and that they do not experience interruptions in service. The staff is using a **Consensogram** to show how ready they are for the move and to create conversations that will help them to prepare.

Bloomfield Breaks the Logjam of Consortium Automation Problems

The Bloomfield-Eastern Greene County Public Library belongs to a shared catalog consortium. The library's circulation, patron registration, and online catalog—and those of the other thirty or so small public and school libraries who participate in the consortium—had been provided by one automation vendor for several years. When the vendor could not provide web-based access or a Windows-based operating system, the consortium made the difficult decision to switch vendors.

Migrating to the new system created a flurry of problems for every library; the problems were exacerbated by the geographic distances, independent boards, and a shortage of local (and consortial) technical expertise. To make matters worse, the libraries were prohibited from seeking technical support directly from the vendor, which insisted that they route all requests through the consortium staff person. The libraries were struggling to cope with a system that couldn't perform basic functions, while their customers became more and more frustrated. The consortium staff person dreaded every phone call that would add to her seemingly endless trouble-shooting. The vendor's technical staff struggled to cope with the stream of issues that arrived from the consortium every day.

After attending a session where they learned to use contin-uous improvement tools, the Bloomfield director worked with the consortium staff member to create a survey of participating libraries. First, the two created a *Check Sheet* of all the problems that had been reported. Using *Nominal Group Technique* via e-mail, they asked the libraries to prioritize the problems that they felt were important to resolve. When the surveys returned, they totaled the number of problems checked, computed the percent of libraries which checked each problem, and then created cumulative percentages. They discovered a strong consensus among the group on which problems were important. Their *Pareto Chart* showed that by addressing a few issues critical to the largest percentage of participating libraries, they could resolve 80 percent of the problems. When they presented the results at the next consortium meeting, the members gave them a standing ovation.

The consortium *Chartered* teams to work on the top three problems in typical consortial style. One library volunteered to dedicate its circulation staff person to developing a procedure manual for circulation.

"Life shrinks or expands in proportion to one's courage."
—attributed to Anaïs Nin

Several other libraries had volunteers who offered to assist with this project. The second area of concern was the inability to get statistical reports. One library had a staff person who had already spent considerable time with this problem and had consulted a university staff person responsible for reports. With his leadership, staff from the consortium and five other libraries met to review what he had developed. When formats were approved, templates were established and e-mailed to all participants. Reports are still not easy to use, but consortium members can get the circulation and patron statistics they need. In the third problem area, training, several situations were identified where more training was needed. One of these was technical services. Software training was held, along with a special "cataloging for beginners" class just for consortium users.

In each of the examples, the libraries faced issues or opportunities that were multi-faceted and complex. The continuous improvement tools allowed them to involve their customers and staff, identify root causes, focus the work on processes instead of personalities, decide where to work, and organize to work efficiently. For these libraries, improvements came more quickly than they expected, building momentum for further efforts.

Glossary of Continuous Improvement Terms

Constancy of Purpose A statement of the library's aim, including its mission, vision, values, and high-level measures.

Customers The recipients of outputs (products or services) of a process or system. May be external (patrons) or internal (other departments).

Key Success Factors Goals and objectives that are critical to the library's fulfilling its mission, reaching its vision, and remaining true to its values.

Mission The library's purpose, the reason it exists.

Process A series of related tasks that transform inputs into outputs. Many processes linked together form a system.

Process Master A document developed in a formal method by the people who do the work, which links customer needs, process controls, and supplier deliveries, so everyone will understand why and how to do the process steps using the most effective current method.

Suppliers Providers of inputs into the process or system.

System A series of related processes linked together to accomplish the aim of the library.

Task A single action, many of which joined together form a process.

Values The shared principles by which the library operates.

Variation The fluctuation inherent in processes. Common cause variation is predictable and normal. Special cause variation is not within predicted limits and is usually caused by extraordinary events.

Vision A vivid picture of the unrealized perfect state to which the library aspires.

Further Reading

Print

Conzemius, Anne and Jan O'Neill. *Handbook for SMART School Teams*. Bloomington, Ind.: National Educational Service, 2002.

Deming, W. Edwards. *New Economics for Industry, Government, Education*, 2nd edition. Cambridge, Mass.: MIT Press, 2000.

-----. *Out of the Crisis*. Cambridge, Mass.: MIT Press, 1982.

Ishikawa, Kaoru. *Guide to Quality Control*. White Plains, N.Y.: Kraus International Publications, 1986.

McConnell, John. *Analysis and Control of Variation*. Manly Vale, NSW, Australia: Delaware Books, 1987.

Sashkin, Marshall and Kenneth J. Kiser. *Putting Total Quality Management to Work; What TQM Means, How to Use It, and How to Sustain It over the Long Run*. San Francisco: Berrett-Koehler Publishers, 1993.

Schaude, G. R. "Methods of idea generation," in S. Gryskiewicz (ed.), *Proceedings of Creativity Week 1, 1978*. Greensboro, N.C.: Center for Creative Leadership, 1979.

Senge, Peter. *Fifth Discipline: The Art and Practice of the Learning Organization*. New York: Doubleday, 1990.

Senge, Peter, A. Kleiner, C. Roberts, et al. *Fifth Discipline Fieldbook: Strategies and Tools for Building a Learning Organization*. New York: Doubleday, 1994.

Shiba, Shoji, Alan Graham, and David Walden. *New American TQM; Four Practical Revolutions in Management*. Portland, Ore.:

Productivity Press, 1993.

Tool Time: Choosing and Implementing Quality Improvement Tools. Molt, Mont: Langford International, 2001.

Wheeler, Donald J. and David S. Chambers. *Understanding Statistical Process Control*, 2nd edition. Knoxville, Tenn.: SPC Press, 1992.

Wilson, Ray W. and Paul Harsin. *Process Mastering; How to Establish and Document the Best Known Way to Do a Job.* New York: Quality Resources, 1998.

Web Sites

Public Sector Improvement Site, Clemson University. deming.eng.clemson.edu/pub/psci

American Society for Quality. www.asq.org

Curious Cat Connections. www.curiouscat.com

Malcolm Baldrige National Quality Award. www.quality.nist.gov

Mt. Edgecumbe High School. www.mehs.educ.state.ak.us/quality/qresources

"We don't need more strength or more ability or greater opportunity. What we need is to use what we have."
—Basil S. Walsh

Sara Laughlin is president of Sara Laughlin & Associates, which specializes in customer-focused, future-oriented planning and communications. Her twenty-five years experience includes seventeen in Indiana library networks. Sara was the architect of the INCOLSA Wheels courier service. In the last five years she has written grants totaling $13 million for Indiana libraries and schools. She is the Continuous Improvement Initiative's library expert.

Denise Sisco Shockley is a library media specialist. She has worked in middle and high school settings, where she was a leader in integrating information literacy and technology into the curriculum. She is educational consultant, project manager, and web designer for the Continuous Improvement Initiative.

Ray Wilson is a process engineer with more than twenty-five years of experience. He is the author of *Process Mastering; How to Establish and Document the Best Known Way to Do a Job* (Quality Resources, 1998). He is an active member of the Indy Quality, Productivity, and Improvement Council and contributes his knowledge and experience with process improvement, as well as tools and techniques, to the Continuous Improvement Initiative.